Cracking MATHS

6th Class Pupil's Book

Brian O'Doherty

gill & macmillan
g&m
primary

Gill & Macmillan
Hume Avenue
Park West
Dublin 12
www.gillmacmillan.ie

ISBN: 978 07171 53893

Design: Design Image and Richard Jervis
Internal illustrations: Kate Shannon
Technical drawings: Design Image
Cover illustration: www.designbos.ie
Consultant editor in mathematics curriculum and pedagogy: Betty Stoutt
Mathematics consultant: Oliver Hyde

The paper used in this book is made from the wood pulp of managed forests. For every tree felled, at least one tree is planted, thereby renewing natural resources.

Any links to external websites should not be construed as an endorsement by Gill & Macmillan of the content or view of the linked material.

For permission to reproduce photographs, the author and publisher gratefully acknowledge the following:
© Alamy: 215; © Getty Images: 144; © Shutterstock: 14, 15, 27, 37, 41, 69, 70, 91, 126, 158, 212, 216;
© Shutterstock/Chris Howey: 125; © Shutterstock/Christian Bertrand: 29.

The author and publisher have made every effort to trace all copyright holders, but if any has been inadvertently overlooked we would be pleased to make the necessary arrangement at the first opportunity.

The author would like to acknowledge the significant contribution made by Aoife Travers in the development of these materials.

	Unit	Strand	Page
1.	**Look Back**		2
2.	Place Value	Number	10
3.	Operations 1	Number	27
4.	Number Theory 1	Number	32
5.	Lines and Angles	Shape and Space	37
6.	Representing and Interpreting Data 1	Data	48
7.	Fractions 1	Number	53
8.	**Check-up 1**	**Revision**	*
9.	2-D Shapes 1	Shape and Space	66
10.	Operations 2	Number	72
11.	Chance	Data	80
12.	Fractions 2	Number	85
13.	2-D Shapes 2	Shape and Space	91
14.	Number Theory 2	Number	101
15.	Equations	Algebra	105
16.	**Check-up 2**	**Revision**	*
17.	Decimals	Number	112
18.	Money	Measures	121
19.	Rules and Properties	Algebra	128
20.	Length	Measures	136
21.	3-D Shapes	Shape and Space	149
22.	Percentages	Number	154
23.	Averages	Data	168
24.	**Check-up 3**	**Revision**	*
25.	Directed Numbers	Algebra	173
26.	Weight	Measures	181
27.	Representing and Interpreting Data 2	Data	188
28.	Area 1	Measures	192
29.	Capacity	Measures	202
30.	Time	Measures	210
31.	Area 2	Measures	217
32.	**Check-up 4**	**Revision**	*

*Access all Check-ups on our website

1. Round these numbers to the nearest hundred.

   a) 78   b) 169   c) 147   d) 236   e) 595

   f) 763   g) 1178   h) 2643   i) 7959   j) 9981

2. Round these numbers to the nearest thousand.

   a) 3512   b) 2456   c) 6219   d) 7632   e) 9884

   f) 12370   g) 18504   h) 27268   i) 22491   j) 39627

3. Estimate the answers to these and then work out the answers to see how accurate your estimate was. Use your calculator to check your answers.

   a)   296   b)   612   c)   1593   d) 3786   e)   2813   f)   8878
         108   289   610   2895   9089   4197
   +   352   +   349   +   1854   + 6378   +   2752   +   5369
   _____   _____   _____   _____   _____   _____

   _____   _____   _____   _____   _____   _____

   g) 6012   h) 8501   i) 4224   j) 8105   k) 15832   l) 27342
   −   2984   −   5367   −   3559   −   3967   −   9685   −   18586
   _____   _____   _____   _____   _____   _____

   _____   _____   _____   _____   _____   _____

4. Circle the prime numbers in the following list.

   | 81 | 17 | 29 | 1 | 36 | 71 |
   | 53 | 57 | 91 | 39 | 41 | 87 |

5. List all the factors of the following numbers.

   a) 16   b) 20   c) 32   d) 40   e) 28   f) 56

6. Find the common factors of the following pairs of numbers.

   a) 9 and 12   b) 16 and 24   c) 18 and 30

   d) 24 and 32   e) 30 and 45   f) 36 and 48

7. List the first 8 multiples of the following numbers.

   a) 3   b) 5   c) 12   d) 9   e) 10   f) 6

8. Draw examples of each of the following.

   a) parallel lines
   b) acute angle
   c) oblique line
   d) right angle
   e) perpendicular lines
   f) obtuse angle
   g) horizontal line
   h) reflex angle
   i) vertical line
   j) straight angle

9. Estimate the size of each of these angles and then check your estimate by measuring them using your protractor.

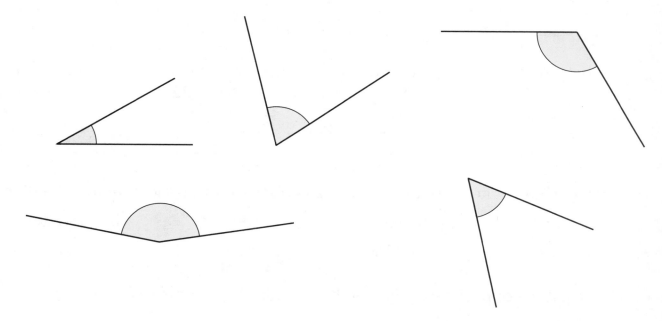

10. Draw these angles using a pencil, ruler and protractor.

    a) 60°   b) 140°   c) 35°   d) 125°

When drawing angles, **remember:**
- Draw one line of the angle with a ruler.
- Place the baseline of the protractor on this line, with the centre point on the end of the line.
- Follow the scale to the angle you want and mark this point.
- Join this point to the end of your line.

11. Estimate the answers before multiplying. Check your answers with a calculator.

	a)	b)	c)	d)	e)	f)
	192	178	127	173	213	358
×	6	9	15	17	23	36

12. Try these. Remember, the first part of your answer will be in the tens column, so you will be estimating by multiplying by a 10 (there could be remainders).

a) $518 \div 14$ b) $342 \div 18$ c) $495 \div 24$

d) $812 \div 28$ e) $630 \div 35$ f) $875 \div 39$

g) hrs	mins		h) hrs	mins		i) hrs	mins		j) hrs	mins
2	27		4	39		3	54		1	35
1	36		2	43		5	26		6	29
+ 3	24		+ 1	16		+ 3	09		+ 2	18

k) hrs	mins		l) hrs	mins		m) hrs	mins		n) hrs	mins
4	23		8	14		6	32		7	05
− 1	49		− 4	56		− 2	45		− 5	18

13. See if you can write these times in the 24-hour system. (Remember to use 4 digits.)

a) 4:34pm b) 8:51am c) 10:19pm d) 11:47am

e) 7:28pm f) 12:37pm g) 1:38am h) 8:06pm

14. Now try it the opposite way. Remember to identify the times as am or pm.

a) 17:05 b) 10:17 c) 23:12 d) 12:15

e) 17:39 f) 03:56 g) 21:42 h) 00:45

15. Find equivalent fractions for the following fractions by multiplying by a member of the family of 1.

a) $\frac{1}{4}$ b) $\frac{1}{8}$ c) $\frac{2}{3}$ d) $\frac{3}{5}$ e) $\frac{7}{10}$ f) $\frac{5}{6}$ g) $\frac{3}{7}$ h) $\frac{5}{9}$

16. Now find equivalent fractions for the following fractions by dividing by a member of the family of 1.

a) $\frac{21}{24}$ b) $\frac{18}{27}$ c) $\frac{14}{18}$ d) $\frac{24}{30}$ e) $\frac{49}{63}$ f) $\frac{32}{56}$ g) $\frac{35}{45}$ h) $\frac{25}{50}$

17. Now try these. Remember to change the fractions so that they have the same denominator. Estimate the answers first.

a) $\frac{1}{2}+\frac{1}{3}$ b) $\frac{1}{4}+\frac{3}{8}$ c) $\frac{2}{3}+\frac{1}{5}$ d) $\frac{1}{8}+\frac{5}{6}$ e) $\frac{3}{4}+\frac{2}{3}$ f) $\frac{5}{12}+\frac{3}{8}$

18. See if you can work these out. Remember to find the lowest common multiple (LCM) of the denominators so that you can make equivalent fractions with the same denominator.

a) $\frac{9}{10}-\frac{3}{4}$ b) $\frac{5}{6}-\frac{2}{9}$ c) $\frac{7}{8}-\frac{5}{6}$ d) $\frac{8}{9}-\frac{1}{6}$ e) $\frac{4}{5}-\frac{3}{4}$ f) $\frac{6}{7}-\frac{2}{3}$

19. Change these mixed numbers into fractions.

a) $1\frac{4}{5} = \frac{}{5}$ b) $1\frac{7}{9} = \frac{}{9}$ c) $2\frac{3}{4} = \frac{}{4}$ d) $3\frac{1}{3} = \frac{}{3}$

e) $2\frac{5}{6} = \frac{}{6}$ f) $4\frac{3}{4} = \frac{}{4}$ g) $6\frac{3}{8} = \frac{}{8}$ h) $7\frac{7}{10} = \frac{}{10}$

20. Change these improper fractions to mixed numbers.

a) $\frac{16}{5}$ b) $\frac{21}{4}$ c) $\frac{19}{3}$ d) $\frac{27}{8}$ e) $\frac{41}{10}$ f) $\frac{46}{7}$ g) $\frac{53}{6}$ h) $\frac{62}{9}$

21. Add the following mixed numbers.

a) $1\frac{1}{2} + 1\frac{1}{4}$ b) $2\frac{1}{3} + 1\frac{1}{5}$ c) $3\frac{1}{6} + 1\frac{3}{4}$

d) $4\frac{2}{3} + 2\frac{3}{4}$ e) $3\frac{3}{4} + 2\frac{5}{6}$ f) $4\frac{3}{8} + 1\frac{5}{6}$

22. Find the difference between the following mixed numbers.

a) $2\frac{5}{6} - 1\frac{2}{3}$ b) $3\frac{7}{8} - 1\frac{1}{6}$ c) $4\frac{7}{8} - 3\frac{5}{6}$

d) $6\frac{2}{3} - 3\frac{3}{8}$ e) $5\frac{4}{5} - 4\frac{1}{4}$ f) $7\frac{8}{9} - 2\frac{1}{6}$

23. Find:

a) $\frac{1}{3}$ of €267   b) $\frac{1}{5}$ of €975   c) $\frac{1}{8}$ of €528

d) $\frac{5}{6}$ of €654   e) $\frac{3}{4}$ of €1976   f) $\frac{5}{9}$ of €2592

24. Work out the whole amount if:

a) $\frac{1}{4} = €238$ b) $\frac{2}{3} = €694$ c) $\frac{4}{5} = €516$

d) $\frac{5}{6} = €765$ e) $\frac{3}{8} = €1941$ f) $\frac{6}{7} = €3234$

25. Change these fractions to decimals.

a) $\frac{1}{10}$ b) $\frac{9}{100}$ c) $\frac{13}{100}$ d) $\frac{48}{100}$

e) $\frac{3}{1000}$ f) $\frac{28}{1000}$ g) $\frac{329}{1000}$ h) $\frac{70}{1000}$

26. Write these decimals as fractions.

a) 0.03   b) 0.007   c) 0.9   d) 0.159   e) 0.27   f) 0.601

27. Find the sum of these decimals.

a) $0.59 + 83.7 + 4.862$ b) $9.47 + 27.8 + 436.9$ c) $3.198 + 39.28 + 643.6$

d) $43.782 + 0.586 + 81.4$ e) $384.27 + 8.15 + 79.826$ f) $6.902 + 19.894 + 286.7$

28. Find the difference between these decimals.

a) $8.14 - 6.7$ b) $49.25 - 38.179$ c) $902.1 - 57.85$

d) $30.04 - 8.168$ e) $3.19 - 0.736$ f) $92.315 - 58.576$

29. Find the product of these decimals.

    a) 1.47×8 b) 71.28×6 c) 4.528×9

    d) 58.06×14 e) 9.581×24 f) 1.675×37

30. Find the quotient of these decimals.

    a) $0.485 \div 5$ b) $8.16 \div 12$ c) $250.6 \div 7$

    d) $49.4 \div 13$ e) $43.01 \div 23$ f) $7.476 \div 28$

31. Express these fractions as percentages.

    a) $\frac{6}{100}$ b) $\frac{14}{100}$ c) $\frac{23}{100}$ d) $\frac{98}{100}$ e) $\frac{11}{100}$ f) $\frac{76}{100}$

32. Express these percentages as fractions.

    a) $64\% = \frac{}{100}$ b) 83% c) 9% d) 56% e) 78% f) 25%

33. Find:

    a) 50% of €86   b) 25% of €192   c) 10% of €7.90

    d) 20% of €385   e) 60% of €9.40   f) 75% of €1188

34. Damian bought a pair of jeans that had a price tag of €56. However, the shop was having a sale and all items were reduced by 25%. What was the sale price of the jeans?

35. Marion bought a painting in an auction for €280 and then sold it on eBay at a profit of 35%. What price did she get for it on eBay?

36. Construct a bar chart showing the favourite subject of those surveyed, represented in the table below.

Subject	History	Music	English	Maths	Gaeilge	PE
Number	28	20	32	40	36	24

37. This table shows the number of rugby matches won by each of the Irish provinces over a period of 2 years. Record the information on a multiple bar chart.

	Leinster	Munster	Connacht	Ulster
2012	30	28	12	22
2013	26	32	16	24

38. Have a go at this 2-D quiz.

a) Why are 2-D shapes called 2-D shapes?

b) What is a polygon?

c) What is the difference between a polygon and a regular polygon?

d) Can you name one example of each?

e) Is this shape a rhombus, a trapezium or a parallelogram?

f) How many lines of symmetry, if any, do the following letters have?

C F H O W Y

g) Draw an example of a tessellating shape pattern.

h) What is a triangle with 2 equal sides called?

39. This robot's face is made up of the nets of 4 different 3-D shapes. Can you name them?

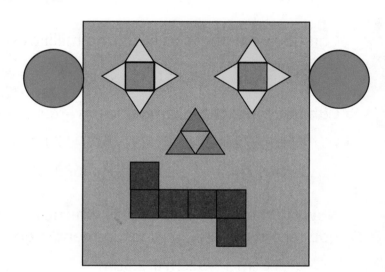

40. Complete the following table.

	No. of flat faces	No. of curved faces	No. of edges	No. of vertices
Cube				
Pyramid				
Cone				
Cuboid				
Cylinder				
Tetrahedron				
Sphere				

41. Fill in the blanks.

    a) 1m 87cm = _____cm

    b) 209cm = ___m _____cm

    c) 3m 45cm = _____m

    d) 5m 3cm = _____m

    e) 2096m = ___km _____m

    f) 8km 752m = _____m

    g) 1.28km = _____m

    h) 984m = _____km

    i) 33mm = ___cm _____mm

    j) 5cm 1mm = _____mm

    k) 9cm 2mm = _____cm

    l) 4.7cm = ___cm _____mm

42. Write these as grams.

    a) 3 kilograms

    b) $1\frac{1}{4}$ kilograms

    c) $3\frac{1}{2}$ kilograms

    d) $\frac{34}{1000}$ kilogram

    e) $\frac{673}{1000}$ kilogram

    f) $5\frac{286}{1000}$ kilograms

43. Write these as kg and g, and also as kg only.

    a) 1967g   b) 3040g   c) 798g   d) 8105g   e) 94g   f) 1850g

44. Can you write these as litres and millilitres?

    a) 5069ml   b) 1.827l   c) 4703ml   d) 5.14l   e) 8957ml   f) 1.8l

45. Can you write these capacities as litres using the decimal point?

    a) 1 litre 572ml

    b) 4170ml

    c) 7 litres 9ml

    d) 3 litres 74ml

    e) 683ml

    f) 8ml

46. Now try these. You can choose whichever way you prefer, but it is very important that you record the unit of measurement in your answer.

    a) 1m 76cm + 482cm + 2.38m

    b) 279m + 3km 49m + 3.19km

    c) 1789g + 3.097kg + 5kg 8g

    d) 3kg 287g + 9.52kg + 786g

    e) 9.357l + 3091ml + $2\frac{1}{4}$l

    f) 3020ml + 5l 78ml + 6.924l

47. The same goes for these.

    a) 82mm – 6.8cm

    b) 7m 9cm – 276cm

    c) 6.25km – 1km 869m

    d) 5l 241ml – 1846ml

    e) 4092g – 2.368kg

    f) 11.3kg – 7kg 459g

48. Have a go at these.

    a) 3km 14m × 9

    b) 6.903l × 6

    c) 7kg 184g × 8

    d) 3.86l × 18

    e) 4m 27cm × 38

    f) 0.846kg × 29

49. Now try these.
    a) 6095ml ÷ 5
    b) 2kg 688g ÷ 7
    c) 2.352km ÷ 12
    d) 11.56l ÷ 17
    e) 15kg 08g ÷ 26
    f) 1km 645m ÷ 35

50. What would be the most appropriate unit of measurement for each of the following?
    a) The distance between London and Paris
    b) The weight of an MP3 player
    c) The amount of water an eggcup would hold
    d) The length of the nib of a pen
    e) The weight of an elephant
    f) The capacity of a water tank
    g) The height of a building
    h) The length of a cucumber

Talk About

1. Here is a number system for you to examine and compare with the number system we use today. The Egyptians had a number system based on hieroglyphs (pictures representing words) from around 3000 BC. Examine the hieroglyphs and try to write the numbers using their symbols.

- The Egyptians had a decimal system using seven different symbols.
- 1 is shown by a single stroke.
- 10 is shown by a drawing of a hobble for cattle.
- 100 is represented by a coil of rope.
- 1000 is a drawing of a lotus plant.

a) 3	b) 9	c) 12	d) 17
e) 21	f) 35	g) 47	h) 54
i) 78	j) 93	k) 170	l) 235
m) 469	n) 531	o) 764	p) 3742

2. Have a go at writing these Egyptian hieroglyphs in our number system. The first two have been done for you.

a) = 3244

b) = 21237

c)

d)

e)

f)

3. See if you can remember how to write these numbers using Roman numerals. For example, 162 = CLXII.

a) 47 b) 95 c) 8 d) 129

e) 273 f) 411 g) 550 h) 688

i) 399 j) 723 k) 743 l) 930

m) 865 n) 1327 o) 3980 p) 2004

4. Convert these Roman numerals to our number system and arrange them in order, starting with the smallest.

a) CCCLVIII, LXXXI, DCCXXXIII, MDXVII, XII

b) MMCCCXXX, III, LXXXIII, MDXV, LXVIII

c) DCLXII, VIII, DCCCXII, MMMCCXXXV, LXXXVIII

As you can see, there is no shorter way of writing, for example, 333 other than CCCXXXIII. The Roman numerals have a specific value and not a **place value**, as in the system we use ourselves.

The system we use today is called the Hindu Arabic number system.

Can you think of any advantages to using our system rather than the two ancient examples above?

The Value of Numbers

List all of the digits we use today, from which all numbers can be made.

0, 1, ____, ____, ____, ____, ____, ____, ____, ____

We use these digits, but to find out what number is being shown depends on the **place value** of the numbers.

For example, what is the value of the 5 in each of these numbers: 5, 50, 500, 5000, 50000?

The digit 5 does not change, but the number depends on where it is **placed**.

1. What is the value of 6 in each of these numbers: ten thousands, thousands, hundreds, tens or units?

a) 36 b) 468 c) 689 d) 45,786 e) 6550

f) 68 g) 65400 h) 10679 i) 2896 j) 456

k) 1674 l) 6 m) 64802 n) 9650 o) 12476

2. Fill in the rest of the number on these notation boards.

a) 24683

T Th	Th	H	T	U
	•• ••			•• •

b) 92345

T Th	Th	H	T	U
		•• •	•• ••	

3. Draw notation boards to show these numbers.

a) 14578   b) 29689   c) 56220   d) 70006   e) 9564

Puzzler

Jennifer was on a train from Paris to Moscow when she spotted a sign saying how many kilometres until the train reached its destination. Somebody stood up in front of her just as they approached the sign, so she couldn't quite read the number properly. She does remember that is was a 4-digit number and that:

- There was a 1 in the number.
- The number in the units was 6 times larger than the number in the tens.
- The number in the hundreds digit was 3.
- The number in the thousands digit was $\frac{1}{3}$ of the number in the ones place.

What was the number?

Now for some larger numbers.

Hundred Thousands

The population of the city Centropolis is 346562, but what does each one of these digits represent?

H Th	T Th	Th	H	T	U
•• •	•• ••	•• •• ••	•• •• •	•• •• ••	••
3	4	6	5	6	2

3 hundred thousands + 4 ten thousands + 6 thousands + 5 hundreds + 6 tens + 2 units

= 300000 + 40000 + 6000 + 500 + 60 + 2

1. Fill in the number 245672 on the notation board.

H Th	T Th	Th	H	T	U
		●● ●● ●			●●

2. Draw notation boards to represent these large numbers.

   a) 179450   b) 560215   c) 245890   d) 438640

3. What is the value of the underlined number (digit)? The first one has been done for you.

   a) 687<u>5</u> = 5 units   b) <u>4</u>5   c) 7<u>5</u>62   d) 2<u>1</u>480

   e) <u>6</u>0179   f) 35<u>8</u>07   g) 789<u>7</u>5   h) 267<u>0</u>

   i) <u>1</u>46320   j) 13<u>5</u>8   k) <u>3</u>11700   l) 5<u>2</u>98

   m) 77<u>7</u>770   n) 8546<u>2</u>   o) 1503<u>1</u>6   p) 624<u>9</u>5

   Why is a digital clock so called?

4. Look at these 6 digits and answer the questions that follow.

   4   2   7   1   0   5

   a) What is the largest number you can make using all 6 digits?
   b) What is the smallest number you can make using all 6 digits?
   c) Write a number using all 6 digits with 7 in the hundreds position.
   d) Write a number using all 6 digits with 1 in the hundred thousands position.
   e) Write a number using all 6 digits with 0 in the units position.
   f) Make the smallest possible even number using all 6 digits.
   g) Make the largest possible odd number using all 6 digits.
   h) Write 3 numbers greater than 720000 using these digits.

5. Expand these numbers. Check your answers with your calculator. The first one has been done for you.

a) 15425 = 10000 + 5000 + 400 + 20 + 5

b) 61202   c) 97055   d) 117890

e) 235004   f) 438693   g) 650431

6. a) Write 5 of your own 6-digit numbers and ask the person beside you to expand them.

b) Have a competition to see who can make the most numbers using these 6 digits. You must use all the digits for each number.

0   3   6   2   8   9

7. Liam and his family are looking to buy a new house. He has been ringing a few estate agents and getting some prices for houses in the area where he wants to live.

Write down the prices in figures and put them in order, starting with the cheapest.

a) One hundred and eighty-five thousand, nine hundred and ten euro

b) Two hundred and sixty thousand, five hundred euro

c) One hundred and seventy thousand, eighty-six euro

d) Four hundred and three thousand, one hundred and twenty euro

e) Two hundred and ninety-eight thousand and seven euro

f) Three hundred and thirty thousand, six hundred and five euro

g) Two hundred and ten thousand, four hundred euro

h) Design a brochure for your own ideal house and put a selling price on it.

8. Write all of the house prices in figures and put them in order, starting with the most expensive house.

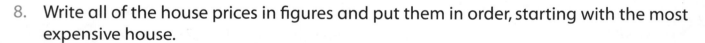

FOR SALE:
4 Bed Detached House €495000

FOR SALE:
4 Bed Detached House €450000

FOR SALE:
2 Bed Semi-detached House three hundred and ninety-five thousand euro

FOR SALE:
2 Bed Semi-detached House three hundred and fifty thousand euro

9. Write these numbers in words.
   a) 1670   b) 13460   c) 55234   d) 178200   e) 340087

10. Christina the car saleswoman is registering 10 new cars today. They are to be registered in a few different counties and Christina rings you to get the information she needs. Write down the registration numbers accurately for her.
    a) One four one L, one hundred and twelve thousand, six hundred and thirty-five
    b) One four one W, seven thousand and eighty-two
    c) One four one MO, four thousand, nine hundred and sixty-two
    d) One four one G, twenty-six thousand, three hundred and thirty-seven
    e) One four one C, eighty thousand, four hundred and seven
    f) One four one DL, seventeen thousand, one hundred and fifty-eight
    g) One four one D, one hundred and twelve thousand, six hundred and thirty-six
    h) One four one WW, eleven thousand, seven hundred and twenty-three

11. Find five real car registration numbers and write them down in words.

12. Here are some groups of 6 random digits. In each case, make the largest number possible; the smallest number possible; three numbers between the smallest and largest.
    a) 2 4 3 6 9 1   b) 8 2 7 5 1 3   c) 7 3 2 6 1 4
    d) 4 2 2 9 5 6   e) 2 7 4 3 7 6   f) 9 8 8 6 6 1
    g) 5 7 2 6 8 4   h) 2 6 9 9 7 5   i) 2 3 5 7 6 8

13. Insert the correct symbol < or > between each of these pairs of numbers.

    a)   23478 _____ 23587

    b)   13540 _____ 12540

    c)   19807 _____ 19708

    d)   30167 _____ 30176

    e)   42590 _____ 42560

    f)   15155 _____ 15150

    g)   67008 _____ 67108

    h)   85600 _____ 80600

    i)   300998 _____ 300898

    j)   676250 _____ 607250

14. Now find the difference between each of the pairs of numbers above.

15. Can you write the next 3 terms in each of these sequences?

    a)   10, 35, 60

    b)   266, 276, 286

    c)   5640, 5540, 5440

    d)   7500, 8500, 9500

    e)   9160, 8160, 7160

    f)   15220, 16220, 17220

    g)   19600, 18500, 17400

    h)   388100, 488100, 588100

Crack the Code

16. You have arrived home and the house alarm is on.

    You can remember the 4-digit code but are not sure of the order of the numbers.

    Here are the 4 digits: **2 5 4 8**.

    Arrange them in as many ways as possible!

17. You have just remembered that your mum told you a way of remembering the alarm code in question 16: it is the greatest odd number you can make with the digits. What is the alarm code?

18. Write these numbers in order starting with the lowest value.

    a)   3507, 305, 3705, 37500, 5037, 35300, 350700, 507, 375300

    b)   18090, 1980, 189000, 9080, 819800, 81900, 8090, 198000

    c)   42500, 5024, 240500, 2450, 54200, 4522, 45240, 425400

    d)   62003, 26003, 30060, 20060, 332500, 632000, 66350, 6023

    e)   97465, 9465, 46599, 5996, 4659, 455900, 555900, 96450

    f)   210378, 2108, 310780, 78310, 7810, 7180, 82100, 210387

19. Work out the sequence and fill in the missing terms.

    a)   1560, 1670, _____, _____, 2000, _____, 2220, _____, _____

    b)   8755, _____, 8505, 8380, _____, _____, 8005, _____, _____, _____

    c)   32100, 33300, 34500, _____, _____, _____, _____, _____

    d)   80300, 65300, _____, _____, _____, _____

    e)   12850, 13000, _____, _____, _____, 13600, _____, _____, _____

Multiplying and Dividing Whole Numbers by 10, 100 or 1000

1. Multiply each of the following numbers by 10, by 100 and by 1000.

    a) 48 b) 92 c) 6 d) 17 e) 25

    f) 176 g) 99 h) 234 i) 541 j) 873

2. Greg's calculator is acting very strangely. When he keys in a number on the screen, it reads as 10 times too big. All of his sums will be wrong, so help him to get the right numbers by dividing each number by 10.

    a) 320 b) 1500 c) 7560 d) 6080

    e) 2550 f) 8200 g) 5710 h) 12450

    i) 367020 j) 754230

    k) Now check your answers on your calculator.

3. Divide each of these numbers by 100.

    a) 1200 b) 3700 c) 18900 d) 63300 e) 159100

Calculating Sequences

Figure out the difference between the first 2 numbers, key it into the calculator and repeatedly press the = sign. Watch what happens!

21350, 20000, _____, _____, _____ ....
21350 – 1350 = 20000
so key in 21,350 – 1350 = = = = to fill in sequence. Try it out!

Note: This may not work on every calculator.

---

4. Use your calculator to complete these sequences.

    a) 12370, 14470, _____, _____, _____, _____, _____, _____

    b) 39200, 37780, _____, _____, _____, _____, _____, _____

    c) 47128, 47817, _____, _____, _____, _____, _____, _____

    d) 78200, 88700, _____, _____, _____, _____, _____, _____

    e) 156300, 152300, _____, _____, _____, _____, _____, _____

    f) 920700, 810700, _____, _____, _____, _____, _____, _____.

Place Value and Decimals

Remember: as with whole numbers, place value is very important when dealing with decimals.

The decimal point separates the whole numbers from the fractions.

In the number 35.412, what does each of the numbers represent?

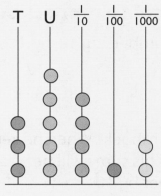

| T | U | $\frac{1}{10}$ | $\frac{1}{100}$ | $\frac{1}{1000}$ |

3   5 · 4   1   2

3 tens + 5 units + 4 tenths + 1 hundredth + 2 thousandths

=   30 + 5 + $\frac{4}{10}$ + $\frac{1}{100}$ + $\frac{2}{1000}$

1. Who has more money?

Tom €12.46

Bill €1.26

2. Who jumped further?

Lisa 4.675m   **Sam 4.576m**

3. Who has the lighter bag?

2.019kg   2.109kg

Gemma   **Aidan**

4. Fill in the following decimal on the notation board: 45.627.

T	U	.	$\frac{1}{10}$	$\frac{1}{100}$	$\frac{1}{1000}$
	▪ ▪ ▪ ▪ ▪ ▪				

5. Draw notation boards to represent each of these numbers.

a) 82.481   b) 20.069   c) 37.705   d) 178.436

e) 360.2   f) 3.971   g) 965.043   h) 1245.62

6. In the following decimals, write down whether the underlined digit is a hundred, ten, unit, tenth, hundredth or thousandth.

a) 45.7̲82   b) 16̲22.8   c) 3.207̲   d) 20̲.061   e) 4.66̲

f) 980.482̲   g) 71̲.002   h) 507.4̲   i) 2.799̲   j) 1̲0.429

k) 2̲67.54   l) 1.9̲   m) 869̲.221   n) 54.07̲3   o) 392.604̲

7. What is the value of the digit 7 in each of these?

a) 179.56   b) 2.875   c) 33.007   d) 714.9

e) 867.05   f) 54.732   g) 890.073   h) 3.217

8. Write these decimals in figures.

a) Three point seven nine two

b) Twenty-five point six eight four

c) Ninety point two four two

d) One hundred and six point zero four nine

e) Four hundred and seventy-two point zero three

f) Eight hundred point seven nine one

g) Fifty-six thousand, three hundred and twelve point eight two

h) Two hundred and thirty-five thousand, five hundred and eight point zero five

9. In the following list, find a) the largest number and b) the smallest number.

2.451, 24.51, 0.245, 245.1, 2.541, 254.1

10. Continue these sequences.

a) 6.1, 6.2, 6.3, _____, _____, _____, _____, _____, _____, _____, _____

b) 19.7, 19.6, 19.5, _____, _____, _____, _____, _____, _____, _____, _____

c) 11.52, 11.53, _____, _____, _____, _____, _____, _____, _____, _____

d) 33.61, 33.63, _____, _____, _____, _____, _____, _____, _____, _____

e) 52.98, 52.88, _____, _____, _____, _____, _____, _____, _____, _____

f) 220.12, 220.16, _____, _____, _____, _____, _____, _____

g) 76.874, 76.875, _____, _____, _____, _____, _____, _____

h) 3.159, 3.158, _____, _____, _____, _____, _____

i) 64.202, 64.204, _____, _____, _____, _____, _____, _____

j) 148.356, 148.456, _____, _____, _____, _____, _____, _____

k) 51.350, 51.348, _____, _____, _____, _____, _____

11. Here is a list of the weight of 8 turkeys ready for Christmas dinner. List the turkeys in order of weight, starting with the heaviest.

3.782kg, 5.907kg, 6.046kg, 5.662kg, 7.81kg, 6.1kg, 4.947kg, 5.97kg

12. List these distances in order, starting with the shortest distance.

Cork – Dublin: 253.15km
Belfast – Limerick: 316.02km
Wicklow – Killarney: 308.517km
Cavan – Tipperary: 209.45km
Sligo – Rosslare: 308.526km
Dublin – Galway: 209.5km
Cork – Belfast: 410.62km
Longford – Waterford: 253.218km

13. Write these decimals in order, starting with the largest.

a) 31.45, 31.512, 31.5, 31.215, 31.1

b) 6.974, 6.879, 6.984, 6.9, 6.891, 7.0

c) 87.62, 86.62, 87.621, 87.601, 87.6

d) 156.2, 156.02, 156.12, 156.22, 156.3

e) 5.902, 5.82, 5.92, 5.913, 5.89

f) 74.82, 74.72, 74.8, 74.71, 74.7, 75.2

14. A comparison was made between a newly released DVD in a few different shops. Put the prices in order, starting with the cheapest.

€29.99, €31.90, €29.90, €30.20, €29.00, €32.50, €31.99, €27.99

15. Round these decimals to the nearest whole unit. (Hint: To the whole unit to which it is closer.)

a)

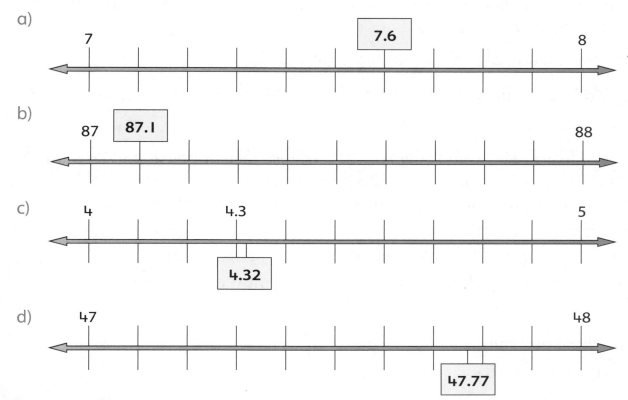

7   7.6   8

b)

87   87.1   88

c)

4   4.3   5
4.32

d)

47   48
47.77

16. What is the nearest whole centimetre to each of the following?

a) 9.2cm

b) 14.7cm

c) 28.1cm

d) 46.5cm

e) 85.8cm

f) 70.3cm

Rounding Numbers to 1 Decimal Place

If you are asked to round a number to 1 decimal place, you must say the tenth that is closest to that number. (Multiples of tenths are 0.1, 0.2, 0.3, 0.4, 0.5, 0.6 and so on.) It helps to look at a number line.

For example: Round 12.47 to one decimal place, i.e. the nearest tenth.

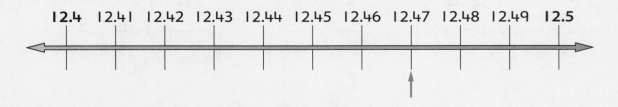

12.4   12.41   12.42   12.43   12.44   12.45   12.46   12.47   12.48   12.49   12.5

Is 12.47 closer to 12.4 or 12.5?

Look at where 12.47 is on the number line. To which tenth is it closer: 12.4 or 12.5?

It is closer to 12.5. Therefore, 12.47 rounds up to the nearest tenth, i.e. 12.5.

When rounding decimals to 1 decimal place, we look at the hundredths. If there are 5 hundredths or more, we increase the tenths by 1. But if there are fewer than 5 hundredths, the tenths stay the same.

For example: Round 12.4<u>7</u> to one decimal place.

The 7 in the hundredths place is greater than 5, so we increase the tenths by 1 = 12.5.

Note:

Numbers 12.41 to 12.44 round down to 12.4 because they are closer to 12.4 than 12.5.
Numbers 12.46 to 12.49 round up to 12.5 because they are closer to 12.5 than 12.4.
Number 12.45 is exactly halfway between 12.4 and 12.5. The rule in this case is to round up to 12.5.

For example: Round 32.6<u>2</u> to 1 decimal place (to the nearest tenth).
The 2 in the hundredths place is less than 5, so the tenths will stay the same = 32.6.

1. Round these decimals to 1 decimal place:

a) 5.28	b) 6.81	c) 9.56	d) 11.29	e) 27.63
f) 32.52	g) 19.96	h) 74.57	i) 40.34	j) 99.96
k) 467.88	l) 515.64	m) 790.33	n) 836.16	o) 820.55
p) 940.99	q) 549.95	r) 1675.43	s) 1789.87	t) 2999.96

Rounding Numbers to 2 Decimal Places

If you are asked to round a number to 2 decimal places, you must say the hundredth that is closest to that number. (Multiples of hundredths are 0.01, 0.02, 0.03, 0.04, 0.05, 0.06 and so on.) It helps to look at a number line.

For example: Round 26.314 to 2 decimal places, i.e. the nearest hundredth.

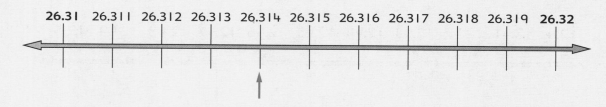

Is 26.314 closer to 26.31 or to 26.32?

Look at where 26.314 is on the number line. To which hundredth is it closer: 26.31 or 26.32?

It is closer to 26.31. Therefore, 26.314 rounds down to the nearest hundredth, i.e. 26.31.

When rounding decimals to 2 decimal places, we look at the thousandths. If there are 5 thousandths or more, we increase the hundredths by 1. But if there are fewer than 5 thousandths, the hundredths stay the same.

For example: Round 26.314 to 2 decimal places.

The 4 in the thousandths place is less than 5, so the hundredths stay the same = 26.31.

Note:

Numbers 26.311 to 26.314 round down to 26.31 because they are closer to 26.31 than 26.32.

Numbers 26.316 to 26.319 round up to 26.32 because they are closer to 26.32 than 26.31.

Number 26.315 is exactly halfway between 26.31 and 26.32. The rule in this case is to round up to 26.32.

For example: Round 56.749 to 2 decimal places.

The 9 in the thousandths place is greater than 5, so the hundredths will increase by 1 = 56.75.

1. Round these decimals to 2 decimal places.

a) 2.526	b) 5.719	c) 4.227	d) 3.762	e) 8.443
f) 11.639	g) 15.725	h) 13.007	i) 19.114	j) 25.608
k) 38.438	l) 65.062	m) 59.558	n) 70.106	o) 47.935
p) 174.122	q) 286.295	r) 193.857	s) 300.866	t) 402.793

2. The butcher cut some pieces of beef that weighed as follows:

a) 1.548kg   b) 0.863kg   c) 2.794kg

d) 1.948kg   e) 2.136kg

The butcher can only fit 2 decimal places on the label of each piece of meat.

Round each weight to 2 decimal places.

Rounding Numbers to 3 Decimal Places

If you are asked to round a number to 3 decimal places, you must say the thousandth that is closest to that number. (Multiples of thousandths are 0.001, 0.002, 0.003, 0.004, 0.005, 0.006 and so on.) It helps to look at a number line.

For example: Round 93.1438 to 3 decimal places, i.e. the nearest thousandth.

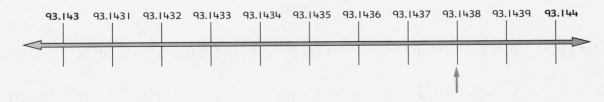

Is 93.1438 closer to 93.143 or to 93.144?

Look at where 93.1438 is on the number line. To which thousandth is it closer: 93.143 or 93.144?

It is closer to 93.144. Therefore, 93.1438 rounds up to the nearest thousandth, i.e. 93.144.

When rounding numbers to 3 decimal places, we look at the ten thousandths. If there are 5 ten thousandths or more, we increase the thousandths by 1. But if there are fewer than 5 ten thousandths, the thousandths stay the same.

For example: Round 93.143<u>8</u> to 3 decimal places (to the nearest thousandth).

The 8 in the ten thousandths place is greater than 5, so we increase the thousandths by 1 = 93.144.

Note:
Numbers 93.1431 to 93.1434 round down to 93.143 because they are closer to 93.143 than 93.144.
Numbers 93.1436 to 93.1439 round up to 93.144 because they are closer to 93.144 than 93.143.
Number 93.1435 is exactly halfway between 93.143 and 93.144. The rule in this case is to round up to 93.144.

For example: Round 11.637<u>4</u> to 3 decimal places.

The 4 in the ten thousandths place is less than 5, so the thousandths will stay the same = 11.637.

1. Round these decimals to 3 decimal places.

a)	3.4468	b)	4.9024	c)	7.1272	d)	1.8936	e)	14.3377
f)	23.4889	g)	37.0341	h)	40.9462	i)	83.5835	j)	71.2864
k)	69.0583	l)	75.5008	m)	89.6331	n)	90.4009	o)	97.1597
p)	156.1384	q)	170.0369	r)	273.1227	s)	428.1444	t)	500.7648

Homework

1. What is the value of 2 in each of these numbers: ten thousands, thousands, hundreds, tens or units?

   a) 427   b) 1298   c) 512   d) 29,045   e) 12670

   f) 154209   g) 42331   h) 62   i) 210386   j) 2908

2. Draw notation boards to represent these large numbers.

   a) 179450   b) 560215   c) 245890   d) 438640

3. Make the largest and smallest numbers possible with the following sets of digits.

   a) 3, 7, 1, 9, 2   b) 4, 0, 2, 5, 8   c) 2, 7, 9, 8, 3, 5

4. Expand these numbers. Check your answers with your calculator.

   a) 27186   b) 39540   c) 61823

   d) 541367   e) 804624   f) 720582

5. Write these numbers in words.

   a) 14206   b) 8031   c) 89213   d) 475920   e) 109604

6. Insert the correct symbol < or > between each of these pairs of numbers.

   a) 13523 _____ 15323   b) 10036 _____ 10306   c) 22124 _____ 21424

   d) 49159 _____ 45199   e) 28110 _____ 28101   f) 63363 _____ 66336

   g) 82546 _____ 82645   h) 58208 _____ 85208   i) 317952 _____ 317592

   j) 843348 _____ 843438

7. Complete these sequences by filling in the next 2 terms.

   a) 1490, 1640, 1790, 1940, _____, _____

   b) 6780, 6690, 6600, 6510, _____, _____

   c) 25400, 25900, 26400, 26900, _____, _____

   d) 71900, 73100, 74300, 75500, _____, _____

   e) 116450, 120450, 124450, 128450, _____, _____

8. Multiply each of the following numbers by 10m, by 100 and by 1000.

   a) 74   b) 86   c) 123   d) 5   e) 182

   f) 320   g) 218   h) 47   i) 736   j) 924

9. Divide these numbers by 10 and by 100.
   a) 3800   b) 29000   c) 238700   d) 3700   e) 10000
   f) 61000   g) 215400   h) 8000   i) 728000   j) 94200

10. Draw notation boards to represent each of these numbers.
    a) 3.209   b) 325.7   c) 34.187   d) 267.102   e) 206.52   f) 84.915

11. In the following decimals, write down whether the underlined digit is a hundred, ten, unit, tenth, hundredth or thousandth.
    a) 7_15.438   b) 29.0_17   c) 80._23   d) 1_6.8   e) _402.954
    f) 47.26_1   g) _9.002   h) 354._896   i) _902.43   j) 6.2_4

12. Place these sets of decimal numbers in order, starting with the smallest.
    a) 2.681, 6.281, 8.261, 1.286   b) 59.24, 52.94, 45.92, 54.29
    c) 1.302, 1.203, 1032, 1.023   d) 21.458, 24.158, 21.854, 21.584

13. Round these decimals to 1 decimal place.
    a) 6.34   b) 8.19   c) 2.27   d) 36.82   e) 80.26
    f) 73.08   g) 9.51   h) 98.43   i) 51.47   j) 127.92

14. Round these decimals to 2 decimal places.
    a) 5.158   b) 2.334   c) 8.706   d) 9.119   e) 6.573
    f) 14.634   g) 29.757   h) 38.129   i) 50.272   j) 66.981

Recap

- I can read, write and order whole numbers.   ◯ ◯ ◯

- I can multiply and divide whole numbers by 10/100/1000.   ◯ ◯ ◯

- I can read, write and order decimals.   ◯ ◯ ◯

- I can round decimals to the nearest unit/1/2/3 decimal places.   ◯ ◯ ◯

Talk About

1. At the school fair, one of the most popular stalls was the one where you guess the number of sweets in the jar. The person who guessed the exact number of sweets would win the jar of sweets. If nobody guessed the exact amount, then the person who made the closest estimate would win. Some people made guesses that were not very close, but most people made very good guesses.

   a) How could you make sure that you made a good guess?
   b) What factors should you take into consideration?
   c) Is it possible to count all of the sweets to make sure you're right?
   d) Make a guess yourself.

2. For the first 4 days of the week, the attendance at a school was as follows:

   Monday – 163   Tuesday – 145   Wednesday – 135   Thursday – 157

   a) Estimate the total attendance for the 4 days.

   b) If you ignore the tens and the units and just focus on the hundreds, what would your estimate be? Would this be an accurate estimate? Give a reason for your answer.

   c) Is 163 closer to 100 or 200? If you round each of the numbers up or down to the nearest hundred, what would your estimate be? Is this a better estimate than your first estimate? Why?

   d) Focus on the tens and units this time. Can you combine them to make hundreds? If you can, what would your estimate be?

   e) This time, focus on the units to see if you can combine them into tens. Then focus on the tens to see if you can combine them into hundreds. Based on these combinations, what would your estimate be?

   f) This time, choose a number (one that's easy to work with) around which the other numbers are spread (clustered). Now multiply that number by the number of days to get a new estimate.

   g) Now add the attendance of each of the days to get the total attendance. Compare the answer to your estimates.

Estimating and Calculating Sums

1. Make the best estimate you can for the following addition sums. Choose whichever method of estimating you prefer.

   a) 2487 + 1729 + 4234 + 7520   b) 913 + 1105 + 6349

   c) 28 + 142 + 1969 + 12856   d) 16908 + 7089

   e) 745 + 2690 + 1261   f) 478 + 512 + 520 + 491

   g) Now use your calculator to calculate the total of each sum. Compare the answer to your estimate.

2. Use your calculator to work out the answers to these.

a)	b)	c)	d)	e)	f)
4985	9158	11,907	19138	8309	23966
7083	12775	15048	18560	28739	31059
+ 2680	+ 8056	+ 3763	+ 21524	+ 14833	+ 28644

g)	h)	i)	j)	k)	l)
33572	20759	37883	43056	37225	51578
25297	21604	41478	37712	47038	29663
+ 38474	+ 33031	+ 26339	+ 23563	+ 43886	+ 46716

3. In a recent vote to decide whether cats should be banned from driving cars, 13597 said that they should be banned, 9711 said that they shouldn't and 3819 said that they had no opinion. How many people voted in total?

4. On a trip to Australia, Tom flew 4759km to Mumbai, where the plane refuelled, and then flew a further 3465km to Sydney. What was the total length of the plane journey?

Puzzler

Estimate the number of children in the school whose first name begins with C.

Use the names of the people in your own class as a way of making a good guess.

Survey all the classes in the school to see what the exact number is.

Did anyone get it right?

Serious Savings

5. This table shows the amount of money saved by some people in their bank accounts over a period of 2 years. Work out how much money each person has saved.

Account Holder	Savings Year 1	Savings Year 2	Total Savings
Mr Eric Euro	€4097	€6395	?
Ms Penny Rich	€7832	€9518	?
Mr Sid Cent	€10284	€6992	?
Ms Mary Moola	€19116	€14577	?
Mr Des Dosh	€21396	€24625	?
Ms Delia Dollar	€33698	€29448	?
Mr Peter Shilling	€37711	€45339	?
Ms Elsie Tanner	€53069	€49413	?

6. The world-famous superhero Centipede Girl recently released her autobiography, *One Leg Ahead of the Rest*. In the first week it sold 14736 copies. In the second week it sold 12965 copies. In the third week it sold 8827 copies. This resulted in the book becoming the number one bestseller in non-fiction. How many copies were sold altogether?

Estimating and Calculating Differences

1. 8987 adults attended a concert. If 3409 were men, estimate how many women attended the concert.

   a) Round up or down to the nearest thousand and make an estimate.

   b) Round up or down to the near est hundred and make an estimate.

   c) Round up or down to the nearest ten and make an estimate.

   d) Which estimate will be the most accurate? Why?

2. Estimate the answers to these.

a) 7509	b) 9788	c) 11611	d) 15908	e) 16348	f) 22167
− 4390	− 2203	− 4390	− 12475	− 9452	− 18643

g) 6901 – 1998

h) 15361 – 2421

i) 10492 – 7105

j) 19282 – 17817

k) 20003 – 13995

l) 28167 – 23579

m) Now work out the answers with a calculator to see how accurate your estimates were.

3. If a man had 4732 daffodils growing in his garden and a dog came in and either ate or destroyed 1857 of them, how many daffodils did the furious man have left in his garden?

4. A woman had saved €6594 after 1 year. At the end of the second year, she had €11415 in her bank account. How much money did she save in the second year?

5. The population of Mars increased from 14271 in the year 2052 to 23806 in the year 2060. By how much did the population increase?

6. Tommy had 32025 germs inhabiting his nose. When he sneezed, 16687 of the germs shot out. How many germs were left wandering about in his nose?

7. The following table shows the number of people who attended various films in their first 2 weeks in the cinemas.

Film Title	Week 1	Week 2
Ninja Hedgehogs 3	15034	13285
The Loneliest Cow in the World	4228	9567
The Cave of Secrets	16714	10339
Damien the Wonder Duck	11992	14106
A Warlock's Tale	21435	20821
Who Shot Wally?	18905	3813

a) Work out the difference in attendance between the 2 weeks for each film.

b) Which film had the biggest increase in attendance in week 2?

c) Which film had the biggest decrease in numbers attending in week 2?

d) Which film had the least difference (either increase or decrease) between week 1 and week 2?

e) How many more people attended The Cave of Secrets than Ninja Hedgehogs 3 in week 1?

f) Did fewer people watch Damien the Wonder Duck and The Loneliest Cow in the World than A Warlock's Tale and Who Shot Wally? in week 2?

Homework

1. Make the best estimate you can for the following addition sums. Choose whichever method of estimating you prefer.

   a) 1512 + 2709 + 3289 + 1485

   b) 5204 + 792 + 1987

   c) 3428 + 573 + 2024 + 97

   d) 13185 + 5803

   e) 689 + 8312 + 1594

   f) 1021 + 989 + 976 + 1018

   g) Now use your calculator to calculate the total in each sum.

2. Work out the answers to these. Check your answers with a calculator.

a)	b)	c)	d)	e)	f)
7246	8276	12869	23427	9575	34793
5397	7809	17118	16815	34894	28188
+ 1574	+ 5463	+ 5294	+ 25734	+ 18628	+ 26941

3. Estimate the answers to these.

a)	b)	c)	d)	e)	f)
6487	8906	10512	17810	15649	24271
− 3106	− 4387	− 6798	− 13286	− 8351	− 16813

   g) 3108 − 1892

   h) 11453 − 6448

   i) 13796 − 9207

   j) 18288 − 14413

   k) 21007 − 17992

   l) 29231 − 21628

   m) Now work out the answers with a calculator.

4. 43278 people went to watch a rugby match. If 17478 were men and 11593 were women, how many children attended the game?

5. 85198 people live in Sugar Plum City and 92015 people live in Swan Lake City. What's the difference in the populations of the 2 cities?

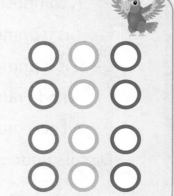

Looking Back at 5th Class

In 5th class we learned that:

factor × factor = product

So in the mathematical sentence $3 × 4 = 12$,

3 and 4 are factors of 12, which is the product. Does 12 have any other factors? What are they?

1. List all the factors of these products.
    a) 9   b) 15   c) 20   d) 24   e) 36   f) 48

A **prime number** is a number whose only factors are itself and 1.
For example, 11 is a prime number because its only factors are 1 and 11.

A **composite number** is a number that has more than 1 pair of factors.
For example, 8 is a composite number because its factors are 1, 2, 4 and 8.

2. True or false?
    a) A factor is one of the numbers in a multiplication question.
    b) factor × factor = product
    c) The only factor a prime number has is 1.
    d) A prime number can be a composite number.
    e) A composite number has more than one pair of factors.
    f) 1 is a prime number.
    g) 2 is a prime number.
    h) All odd numbers are prime numbers.
    i) All even numbers are composite numbers.

    Discuss your answers with the people near you.

3. a) Write down all the odd numbers between 34 and 50.
    b) How many of these numbers are prime numbers?
    c) Now write down all the even numbers between 57 and 71.
    d) What is the sum of the odd numbers between 20 and 30?
    e) How would you know if a number was odd or even if you divided that number by 2?

4. Pick out the prime numbers in the following list of numbers.

23	9	15	17	41	49
37	39	21	67	59	81

5. Find the sum of the prime numbers between 60 and 70.

6. Now pick out the composite numbers in the following list of numbers.

33	19	27	2	45	51
77	25	121	61	11	63

7. Find the sum of the composite numbers between 41 and 47.

8. Make a list of the factors of each of the following numbers. Remember to list all of the factors.
    a) 14   b) 20   c) 16   d) 24   e) 32   f) 40

Highest Common Factors

9. List all of the factors of the following pairs of numbers. Circle the factors that they have in common.
    a) 12 and 18   b) 21 and 28   c) 24 and 36
    d) What's the highest common factor (HCF) in each case?

> The **highest common factor (HCF)** is the biggest number you can divide into a pair of products without having a remainder.

Puzzler

A florist has 56 tulips and 63 roses that she would like to use to create beautiful bouquets.

a) What is the largest number of identical bouquets that she can create without having any leftover flowers?

b) How many tulips and roses will be in each bouquet?

10. Find the highest common factors (HCFs) of each of the following pairs of numbers.

a) 30 and 42   b) 32 and 48   c) 45 and 54

d) 36 and 60   e) 28 and 56   f) 40 and 64

Multiples

1. Use pegboards to help you write down the first 6 multiples of the following numbers. The first one has been done for you – just record the numbers.

    4   7   9   12   15   20

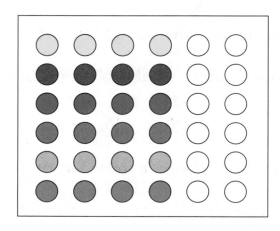

2. Make lists of the following.

a) The first 4 multiples of 11   b) The first 6 multiples of 8

c) The first 3 multiples of 13   d) The first 9 multiples of 3

e) The first 7 multiples of 5   f) The first 5 multiples of 14

3. Pick the odd one out in each of these lists of numbers. Explain your choice.

a) 35, 14, 56, 72, 84, 21   b) 24, 30, 40, 16, 56, 96

c) 21, 12, 33, 18, 27, 35   d) 63, 18, 42, 36, 72, 27

4. Use your calculator to help you figure out the following.

a) Is 1344 a multiple of 6?   b) Is 4976 a multiple of 8?

c) Is 2874 a multiple of 4?   d) Is 6381 a multiple of 9?

e) Is 5743 a multiple of 7?   f) Is 9376 a multiple of 14?

5. Use your calculator to help you do these.

a) Circle the multiples of 3.   198,   746,   2181,   4333

b) Circle the multiples of 11.   605,   908,   1234,   4323

c) Circle the multiples of 7.   345,   854,   1001,   2983

d) Circle the multiples of 12.   648,   1388,   2352,   8766

Lowest Common Multiples

Look at this multiplication question:

$$6 \times 8 = 48$$

We know that 48 is a multiple that is **common** to both 6 and 8, so an easy way to find a **common multiple** of 2 numbers is to multiply the 2 numbers.

But is 48 the first or **lowest common multiple (LCM)** of 6 and 8?

Write out the lists of their multiples. See if you can find a common multiple that is lower than 48.

6: 6, 12, 18, 24, 30, 36, 42, 48
8: 8, 16, 24, 32, 40, 48, 56, 64

The **lowest common multiple (LCM)** will be the first multiple that is on both lists, so the LCM of 6 and 8 is 24.

6. Now find the lowest common multiples (LCMs) of these pairs of numbers.
   a) 6 and 10
   b) 4 and 6
   c) 8 and 12
   d) 8 and 10
   e) 6 and 9
   f) 9 and 12
   g) 5 and 7
   h) 10 and 12
   i) 8 and 9

7. Yes or no?
   a) Is 30 the LCM of 5 and 10?
   b) Is 54 the LCM of 6 and 9?
   c) Is 48 the LCM of 12 and 16?
   d) Is 60 the LCM of 15 and 30?
   e) Is 72 the LCM of 9 and 12?
   f) Is 63 the LCM of 7 and 9?

Homework

1. Put a circle around the prime numbers and a square around the composite numbers in the following list.

   33   49   59   67   81   91

2. List all of the factors of the following numbers.
   a) 16   b) 21   c) 27   d) 30   e) 36   f) 48

3. Find the highest common factor of the following pairs of numbers.
   a) 16 and 24
   b) 20 and 30
   c) 27 and 36
   d) 36 and 48
   e) 24 and 32
   f) 18 and 30

4. List the first 7 multiples of the following numbers.

    a) 3   b) 6   c) 10   d) 13   e) 18   f) 21

5. Find the lowest common multiple of the following pairs of numbers.

    a) 4 and 7   b) 5 and 6   c) 7 and 8

Recap

- I can identify prime and composite numbers.   ○ ○ ○

- I can find the highest common factor of 2 numbers.   ○ ○ ○

- I can find the lowest common multiple of 2 numbers   ○ ○ ○

Talk About

1. Name the lines formed by each of the following objects. Here are a few words to help you:

> horizontal   vertical   oblique   parallel   perpendicular

    a) The lines formed by the wires on the electricity pylon
    b) The sloping lines of the roof of a house
    c) The lines formed at the crossroads
    d) The legs of the table
    e) The table top

2. Find 2 more examples of each type of line in the pictures above.

3. Match the correct name to each line.

> parallel lines   horizontal line   perpendicular lines   oblique line   vertical line

    a)   b)   c)   d)   e)

4. Look around your classroom and name 5 examples of lines or surfaces that are vertical, oblique and horizontal.

5.   a) What would you use to check if surfaces or lines are vertical or horizontal?
    b) When would it be important to ensure that they are horizontal or vertical?
    c) Identify examples of parallel and perpendicular lines on your school building or in the yard. Try to find some examples that others may not identify.

Strand: Shape and Space
Curriculum Objectives:
Recognise, classify and describe angles and relate angles to shape;   estimate, measure and construct angles in degrees;
recognise angles in terms of a rotation;   explore the sum of the angles in a quadrilateral.

Different Types of Angle

> **Remember:** an **angle** is formed when 2 straight lines meet. It is a measure of the rotation formed between the 2 lines and is measured in degrees.
>
> A full rotation is 360° and half a rotation is 180°.

1. What angle is made by perpendicular lines?

2. Draw an example of each type of angle and write a short description of each.

   For example:

   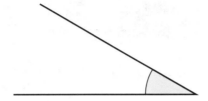

   Acute angle: Measuring between 0° and 90°.

3. Name the angle: acute, right, obtuse, straight, reflex or full rotation.
   - a) 45°
   - b) 90°
   - c) 110°
   - d) 15°
   - e) 268°
   - f) 180°
   - g) 360°
   - h) 92°
   - i) 178°
   - j) 201°
   - k) 3°
   - l) 136°
   - m) Pick 5 of these angles and draw what you think they might look like.

4. Write down your name using only capital letters. Name all of the angles made by the straight lines.

5. On some squared paper, design a house that has no right angles.

6. Can you find an example of each angle on this bicycle?

7. Name all of the angles in these polygons. Are they right angles, acute angles, obtuse angles, straight angles or reflex angles?
   - a)
   - b)
   - c)

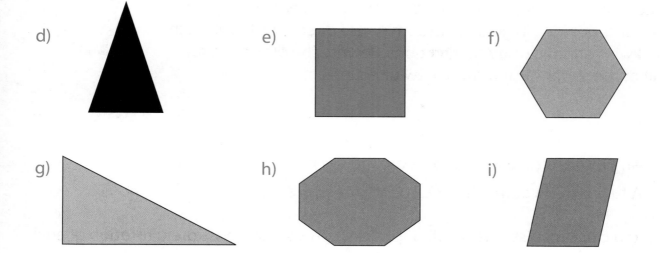

d) e) f)

g) h) i)

8. Can you draw 1 shape that includes each of these angles?

right angle   acute angle   obtuse angle   straight angle

9. Using your tangram pieces, identify the types of angle on each piece and then make a shape using a few pieces to give an example of these angles: reflex, obtuse, acute.

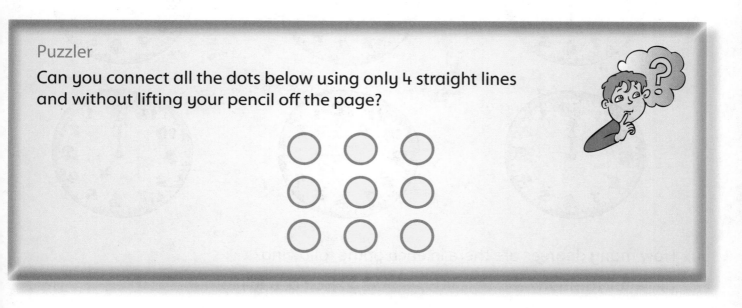

Puzzler

Can you connect all the dots below using only 4 straight lines and without lifting your pencil off the page?

Making Shapes

10. Write a set of instructions for a person to walk in the shape of a square. Use directions such as 'Turn _____° to your left/right. Take 5 steps forwards/backwards', etc. Say this to start: 'Stand up, turn 90° to your right and take 4 steps forward.' Test out your set of instructions with the person beside you.

11. Now write a set of instructions for a person to walk in these shapes: isosceles triangle, parallelogram, large rectangle, hexagon.

12. Instead of using left/right directions, find out where north, south, east and west are in your classroom or use directions to rotate in clockwise or anticlockwise directions. Rewrite the directions for one of the shapes using these new directions.

Angles as Rotations

1. a) Angles are a measure of rotation and are measured in _____.

   b) A full rotation or full turn is _____ degrees, or _____°.

2. Using a clock face, straws or lollipop sticks, can you demonstrate a rotation of each type of angle?

3. Have a look at the following clock faces. What angles are being made by the hands of each clock? Is there more than one angle being made?

a)

b)

c)

d)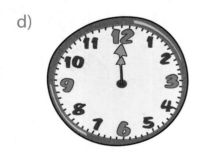

e)

f)

4. How many degrees are there in each of the following?

   a) A full rotation

   b) Half of a full rotation

   c) A quarter of a full rotation

   d) Three-quarters of a full rotation

5. Examine this clock face. If there are 12 numbers on the clock face and there are 360° in a full rotation, then to move from one number to the next, we are moving $\frac{1}{12}$ of a full rotation, which = _____°.

6. Using the information from question 5, answer the following questions.

   a) How many degrees does the hour hand rotate through if it moves clockwise from 1pm to 3pm?

   b) If the hour hand moves clockwise from 5am to 10am, how many degrees does it rotate through?

   c) If the hour hand moves clockwise from 2pm to 11pm, how many degrees does it rotate through?

   d) How many degrees does the hour hand rotate clockwise through from 9pm to 4am?

7. How many degrees will the minute hand of the clock rotate through in each of the following?

   a) 30 minutes   b) 60 minutes   c) 25 minutes   d) 40 minutes

Measuring Angles with a Protractor

1. Estimate the size of each of these angles and then measure them using your protractor. Remember to place the base line of the protractor along one of the lines of the angle and the point of the angle on the centre point of the protractor.

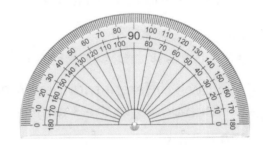

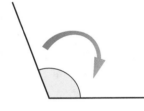      

2. Have a look at this picture and find 5 different angles. Estimate the size of each angle and then measure the angle to check your estimate.

Constructing Angles with a Protractor

1. You have been asked to draw a sketch for a maze in an adventure theme park. Include each of these angles in your maze and construct the angles using your protractor:

    a) 90°

    b) 50°

    c) 65°

    d) 120°

    e) 170°

    f) 140°

    g) 10°

    h) 100°

    i) 180°

    j) 270°

    k) 190°

    l) 295°

2. Construct shapes with the following angles.

    a) Triangle: 55°, 60°, 65°

    b) Square: 90°

    c) Triangle: 27°, 115°, 38°

    d) Triangle: 70°, 40°, 70°

3. Draw 5 reflex angles using your 180° protractor, pencil and ruler. Get the person beside you to measure the angles and write down their size.

The Sum of the Angles of a Triangle

4. Draw 4 different triangles. Measure their angles using a protractor and find their sum. When you add the 3 angles of each triangle, what do you get?

    A + B + C = _____°

    So we can say the sum of the angles of a triangle is _____°.

5. Calculate the missing angles.

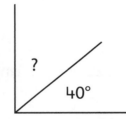 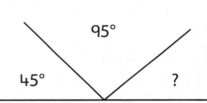

6. From what you know about the sum of the angles of a triangle, can you find the missing angles in these triangles?

    a)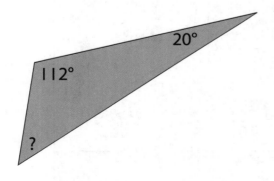

    b)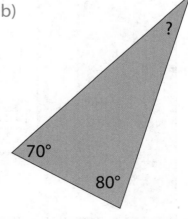

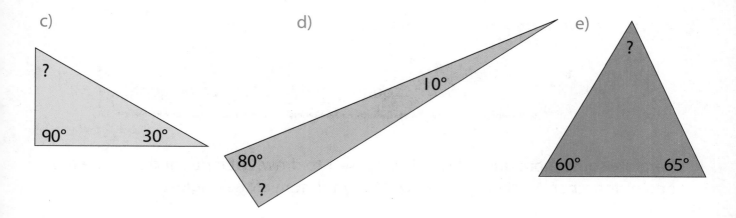

c)

?
90°   30°

d)

10°

80°

?

e)

?

60°   65°

7. Now try these.

a)

85°   115°

?

b)

95°   110°

?

c)

45°   ?

196°

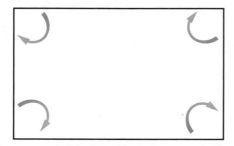

Remember: there are 360° in a full rotation.

8. Draw a rectangle on a piece of paper using a ruler. Cut out the rectangle and mark
    the 4 angles. Tear off the 4 angles and fit them together. What do you notice about
    the angle they make?

The Sum of the Angles of a Quadrilateral

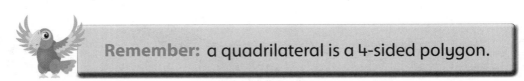

Remember: a quadrilateral is a 4-sided polygon.

1. Here are some more quadrilaterals. Choose 1 to draw. Cut it out and arrange the angles together. What do you notice about the sum of the angles?

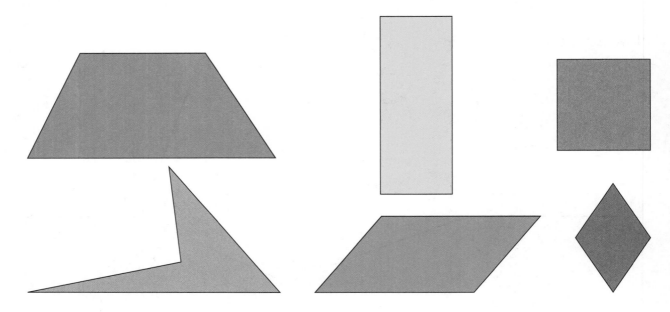

2. Draw 2 more quadrilaterals and measure the angles of each using your protractor. Find their sum.

3. So from what you have found: The sum of the angles of a quadrilateral is _____°.

4. Find the missing angles in these quadrilaterals.

   a)

   b)

   c)

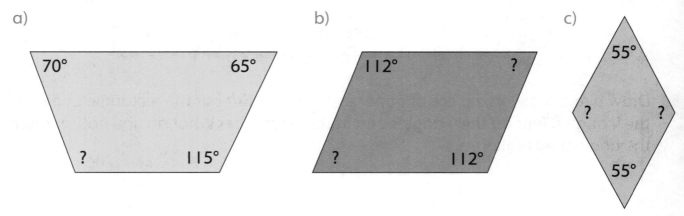

Homework

1. Match each type of line in the list below to its description.

> horizontal   perpendicular   oblique   parallel   vertical

   a) 2 lines that are always the same distance apart

   b) A line that goes straight across

   c) 2 lines that make right angles with one another

   d) A line that goes diagonally

   e) A line that goes straight down from top to bottom

   f) Now draw an example of each type of line.

2. Now match each correct angle in the list below to the correct description.

> acute   straight   right   obtuse   reflex

   a) An angle that is exactly 90°

   b) An angle that is greater than 90° but less than 180°

   c) An angle that is greater than 180° but less than 360°

   d) An angle that is exactly 180°

   e) An angle that is greater than 0° but less than 90°

   f) Now draw an example of each type of angle.

3. Name the angle: acute, right, obtuse, straight or reflex.
   a) 135°   b) 23°   c) 180°   d) 207°
   e) 94°   f) 86°   g) 320°   h) 90°

4. What angles are being made by the hands of each clock? Remember: there is more than 1 angle being made.

   a)

   b)

   c)

d)
e)
f)

5. What fraction of a rotation are the following angles?

   a) 90°   b) 180°   c) 45°   d) 360°   e) 60°

6. Use your protractor to measure the following angles.

   a)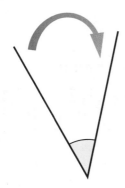

   b)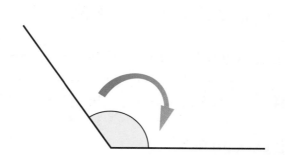

   c)

7. Use your protractor to construct the flowing angles.

   a) 45°   b) 140°   c) 20°   d) 135°
   e) 75°   f) 155°   g) 15°   h) 170°

8. Fill in the missing angles below.

   a)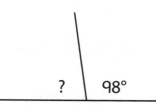

   b)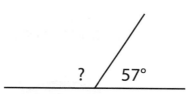

   c)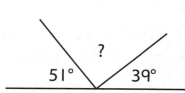

9. Fill in the missing angles from these triangles.

   a) 43°, 78°, ?   b) 107°, 29°, ?   c) 36°, 57°, ?   d) 85°, 47°, ?

10. Now try these.

a)

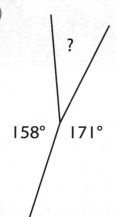

? 158° 171°

b)

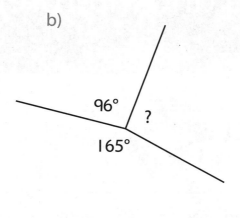

96° ? 165°

c)

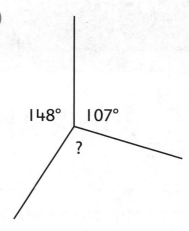

148° 107° ?

Talk About

Data can be collected, organised and represented in a variety of ways. You are already familiar with pictograms, bar charts and multiple bar charts.

1. Carry out an investigation into the pets your classmates have. What questions will you ask? How will you record your information? Display your results on a pictogram.

Dog		Fish	
Cat		Bird	

2. Choose 5 school subjects and interview your class to see which subject is their favourite. Use a tally sheet to record your results and then present your results on a bar chart.

3. Examine this multiple bar chart representing the number of boys and girls in each class from 1st to 6th. Answer the questions that follow.

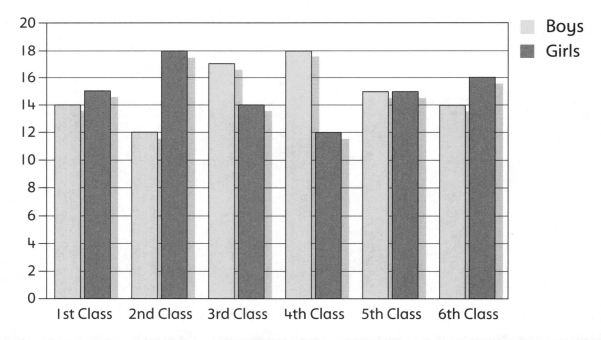

a) Name the classes that have more boys than girls.

b) Name the classes that have more girls than boys.

c) Which class has an equal number of boys and girls?

d) How many boys are in the school from 1st to 6th class?

e) How many more girls than boys are there in the 1st to 6th classes?

f) Carry out a similar investigation in your own school.

Looking at Trend Graphs

1. Examine this **trend graph** showing a newsagent's takings for the week. Answer the questions that follow.

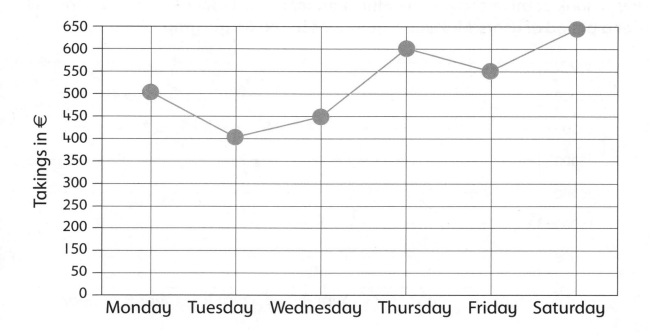

a) Which day had the lowest amount of takings?

b) Which day had the highest amount of takings?

c) Name 2 days in which the takings i) increased and ii) decreased from the day before.

d) How much money was taken in in total by the shop that week?

e) What were the average takings per day?

> A **trend graph** is another way of representing data. In the graph above, we can easily see on which days the takings increased and decreased or the trend of the takings from day to day.

2. Have a look at this trend graph of the number of trucks made by a manufacturer over a period of years. Make up 5 questions based on the graph.

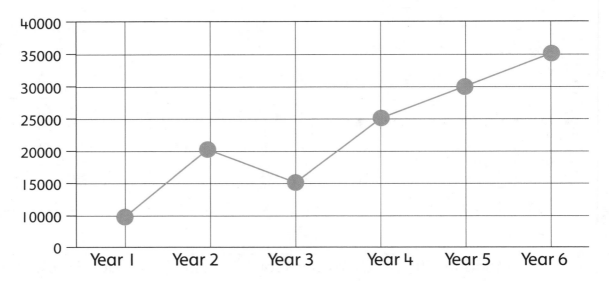

Drawing Trend Graphs

1. Draw a trend graph to display this information about the rainfall over several months. Remember to mark the millimetres of rainfall for each month with a dot and then join the dots with lines to show the trend.

Month	Nov	Dec	Jan	Feb	Mar
Rainfall (mm)	180	240	220	160	200

Answer the following questions once you have drawn your trend graph.

a) In which month did the greatest amount of rain fall?

b) In which month did the least amount of rain fall?

c) Name the months that showed an increase in rainfall.

d) By how much did the rainfall in December exceed that in February?

e) From the graph, can you estimate the average rainfall over these months? Check your estimate by calculating the average.

f) Which months had above average rainfall?

2. Record the temperature at midday for a week. Display your results on a trend graph.

a) Which days showed an increase in temperature?

b) Which days showed a decrease in temperature?

c) What was the average daily temperature for that week?

3. Here are the sales figures of a computer company for the last 6 months of the year. Show this information on a trend graph and write a short account of what the trend shows. Why do you think December shows a large increase in sales?

Month	Sales
July	€40000
Aug	€30000
Sept	€20000
Oct	€30000
Nov	€40000
Dec	€60000

4. Record the attendance of your classmates over 5 schooldays. Display your results on a trend graph.

Homework

1. This table shows the results of a survey to find the favourite fruit of the children in a school. Represent the information on a bar chart. Choose an appropriate scale for the numbers.

Fruit	Apple	Grapes	Banana	Kiwi	Orange
Number of children	45	30	40	25	35

2. This trend graph represents the number of days during which it rained in each of the seasons.

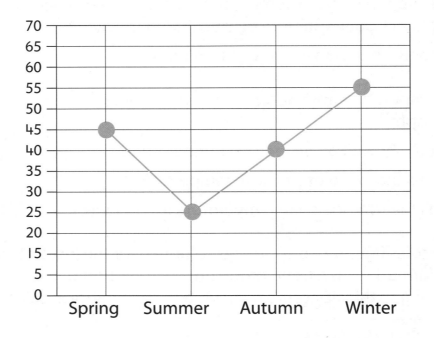

a) Which season had the second highest number of rainy days?

b) Which season had the second lowest number of rainy days?

c) What was the difference in the number of rainy days between the season with the most and the season with the fewest?

d) How many days did it rain throughout the year?

e) What was the average number of rainy days across the 4 seasons?

3. a) Construct a trend graph to represent the following data, which describes the number of children who were absent from school during the course of 1 week.

   b) Make up 5 questions based on your graph.

Day	Mon	Tues	Wed	Thurs	Fri
Number absent	44	36	28	32	40

Recap

- I can represent data in different ways. ○ ○ ○

- I can interpret trend graphs. ○ ○ ○

- I can construct trend graphs. ○ ○ ○

 # Talk About

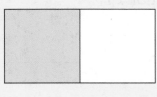 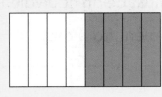

$\frac{1}{2}$ $\frac{4}{8}$

Look carefully at these 2 fraction amounts. What do you notice?

What can we say about $\frac{1}{2}$ and $\frac{4}{8}$?

1. Which of these pairs of fractions are equivalent? Use the fraction wall to help you.

a) $\frac{1}{3}$ and $\frac{1}{2}$ b) $\frac{1}{4}$ and $\frac{2}{8}$ c) $\frac{1}{2}$ and $\frac{4}{9}$

d) $\frac{1}{3}$ and $\frac{3}{8}$ e) $\frac{2}{3}$ and $\frac{4}{6}$ f) $\frac{3}{3}$ and $\frac{9}{9}$

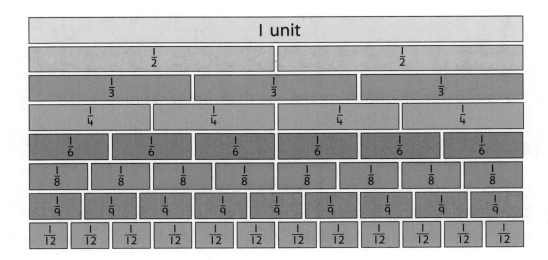

2. Why are all these fractions equivalent?

$\frac{4}{4}$ $\frac{9}{9}$ $\frac{2}{2}$ $\frac{7}{7}$ $\frac{15}{15}$ $\frac{133}{133}$

They are all _____ of the _____ of _____.

Making Equivalent Fractions

$$8 \times 1 = 8$$

When you multiply a number by 1, you don't change the value of the number.

So what happens when you multiply a fraction ($\frac{3}{4}$) by a member of the family of 1 ($\frac{3}{3}$)?

$$\frac{3}{4} \times \frac{3}{3} = \frac{9}{12}$$

Because you are multiplying by 1, you don't change the value of the fraction. That means the answer must be an equivalent fraction of $\frac{3}{4}$.

So $\frac{3}{4}$ and $\frac{9}{12}$ are equivalent fractions.

1. Find equivalent fractions for these by multiplying.

   a) $\frac{2}{5} \times \frac{2}{2}$

   b) $\frac{2}{3} \times \frac{8}{8}$

   c) $\frac{1}{6} \times \frac{4}{4}$

   d) $\frac{5}{9} \times \frac{7}{7}$

   e) $\frac{7}{8} \times \frac{12}{12}$

   f) $\frac{6}{11} \times \frac{3}{3}$

2. Find out which members of the family of 1 were used to make these pairs of equivalent fractions.

   a) $\frac{4}{7} \times - = \frac{12}{21}$

   b) $\frac{3}{8} \times - = \frac{15}{40}$

   c) $\frac{2}{3} \times - = \frac{18}{27}$

   d) $\frac{5}{9} \times - = \frac{35}{63}$

   e) $\frac{3}{10} \times - = \frac{33}{110}$

   f) $\frac{7}{12} \times - = \frac{56}{96}$

$$9 \div 1 = ?$$

If you divide a number by 1, you don't change the number's value.

Likewise, you can divide a fraction ($\frac{5}{10}$) by a member of the family of 1 ($\frac{5}{5}$) to get an equivalent fraction.

$$\frac{5}{10} \div \frac{5}{5} = \frac{1}{2}$$

So $\frac{5}{10}$ and $\frac{1}{2}$ are equivalent fractions.

3. Find equivalent fractions for these fractions by dividing.

   a) $\frac{3}{9} \div \frac{3}{3}$

   b) $\frac{8}{12} \div \frac{4}{4}$

   c) $\frac{15}{20} \div \frac{5}{5}$

   d) $\frac{21}{56} \div \frac{7}{7}$

   e) $\frac{36}{48} \div \frac{12}{12}$

   f) $\frac{45}{72} \div \frac{9}{9}$

You can multiply a fraction by any member of the family of 1 to make an equivalent fraction. But you can divide only by certain members of the family of 1 to make equivalent fractions. Can you suggest why?

$$\frac{6}{9} \div \frac{4}{4}$$

Try to make up a rule for what members of the family of 1 you can divide by to make equivalent fractions. (Hint: You should use the words *common factors*.) Compare your rule with the ones of the people beside you.

4. Now fill in the missing numerators/denominators to make the fractions equivalent. You can do the multiplying and dividing in your head.

a) $\frac{1}{2} = \frac{}{14}$

b) $\frac{2}{3} = \frac{12}{}$

c) $\frac{3}{} = \frac{15}{25}$

d) $\frac{}{6} = \frac{35}{42}$

e) $\frac{7}{9} = \frac{}{81}$

f) $\frac{9}{} = \frac{27}{33}$

g) $\frac{6}{7} = \frac{48}{}$

h) $\frac{5}{} = \frac{35}{49}$

i) $\frac{7}{12} = \frac{}{48}$

j) $\frac{4}{7} = \frac{36}{}$

k) $\frac{3}{} = \frac{27}{90}$

l) $\frac{6}{11} = \frac{}{99}$

Changing Mixed Numbers to Improper Fractions

1. Charlotte the Champion Chocolate Chewer practised by eating $2\frac{4}{5}$ bars of chocolate every day. If there were 5 pieces of chocolate in each bar, how many pieces did she eat altogether each day?

2. Draw the bars and shade the amount of chocolate Charlotte ate. Now count the pieces. Write it as an improper fraction:

$$2\frac{4}{5} = \frac{}{5}$$

3. Now work out how many pieces of chocolate each of these people ate. Draw the bars to help you. You know how many pieces were in each bar from the denominator:

$1\frac{1}{6}$ means 6 pieces in a full bar,

so $1\frac{1}{6} = \frac{7}{6}$.

a) Cherie ate $1\frac{3}{4}$ bars of chocolate

b) Charmaine ate $2\frac{1}{3}$ bars of chocolate

c) Cheryl ate $2\frac{5}{7}$ bars of chocolate

d) Champagne ate $3\frac{2}{5}$ bars of chocolate

> Can you work out a quick way of changing a mixed number into an improper fraction?
> Talk about it with the people near you.

4. Now change these mixed numbers into improper fractions the quick way.

   a) $1\frac{8}{9} = \frac{}{9}$

   b) $2\frac{1}{10} = \frac{}{10}$

   c) $4\frac{3}{4} = \frac{}{4}$

   d) $5\frac{2}{3} = \frac{}{3}$

   e) $4\frac{1}{7} = \frac{}{7}$

   f) $3\frac{3}{8} = \frac{}{8}$

   g) $7\frac{3}{5} = \frac{}{5}$

   h) $6\frac{6}{7} = \frac{}{7}$

   i) $9\frac{5}{9} = \frac{}{9}$

Changing Improper Fractions into Mixed Numbers

Charles was Charlotte's main rival for the Champion Chocolate Chewer's Crown.
He practised by eating 13 pieces of chocolate a day. The bars that he preferred had
4 pieces of chocolate in them. How many full bars and extra pieces did he eat?

Sort the pieces of chocolate into groups of 4. How many full groups of 4 pieces are
there? How many leftover pieces are there? You can write it as a mixed number.

The denominator is always the number of pieces in a full bar, so
$$\frac{13}{4} = 3\frac{1}{4}.$$

A **mixed number** is a number that is made up of
a whole number and a fraction.

1. Now see how many full bars and extra pieces each of these people ate. Draw the
    pieces and sort them to help you.

   a) Chuck ate 15 pieces a day and his bars had 8 pieces in them.

   b) Chad ate 18 pieces a day and his bars had 7 pieces in them.

   c) Chris ate 23 pieces a day and his bars had 9 pieces in them.

   d) Chip ate 21 pieces a day and his bars had 6 pieces in them.

   e) Chandler ate 26 pieces a day and his bars had 3 pieces in them.

   f) Chesney ate 27 pieces a day and his bars had 4 pieces in them.

> What's the quickest way of changing an improper fraction into a mixed number?
> Again, you might like to talk about it with the people around you.

2. Change these improper fractions into mixed numbers the quick way.

a) $\frac{26}{5}$　　b) $\frac{23}{8}$　　c) $\frac{31}{10}$　　d) $\frac{17}{2}$　　e) $\frac{19}{4}$　　f) $\frac{41}{12}$

g) $\frac{54}{7}$　　h) $\frac{96}{11}$　　i) $\frac{45}{8}$　　j) $\frac{29}{3}$　　k) $\frac{61}{9}$　　l) $\frac{47}{6}$

Puzzler

A fraction walked into a shop and asked for a fraction of a kilogram of flour that was exactly double his size. 'I was half expecting you would say that,' said the shopkeeper, 'but I decided to double your order again and give you a full kilogram of flour.' Can you work out the value of the fraction that walked into the shop?

Finding Common Denominators

Which of these fraction amounts is bigger?

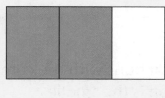 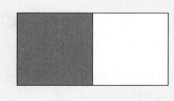

$\frac{2}{3}$ 　　　　 $\frac{1}{2}$

In this case it's pretty obvious, but what if the fraction amounts are very similar?

Which of these fraction amounts is bigger?

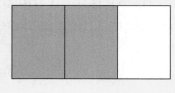 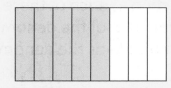

$\frac{2}{3}$ 　　　　 $\frac{5}{8}$

Now it's more difficult to tell.

So which fraction is bigger?

If both fractions had the same denominator, we could tell straight away which was bigger. So we need to find equivalent fractions for $\frac{2}{3}$ and $\frac{5}{8}$ that have the same denominator.

What is the lowest common multiple (LCM) of 3 and 8?

3: 3, 6, 9, 12, 15, 18, 21, 24, 27
8: 8, 16, 24, 32, 40, 48, 56, 64
24 is the LCM.

$$\frac{2}{3} = \frac{16}{24} \qquad\qquad\qquad \frac{5}{8} = \frac{15}{24}$$

So $\frac{2}{3}$ is bigger than $\frac{5}{8}$.

1. Work out which fraction in each of these pairs of fractions is bigger. Change the pairs of fractions so that they have the same denominators to help you.

   a) $\frac{1}{2}$ and $\frac{4}{7}$
   b) $\frac{2}{5}$ and $\frac{1}{3}$
   c) $\frac{3}{4}$ and $\frac{2}{3}$
   d) $\frac{5}{6}$ and $\frac{9}{10}$
   e) $\frac{5}{8}$ and $\frac{7}{10}$
   f) $\frac{3}{8}$ and $\frac{5}{12}$

Which of these 3 fractions is the smallest?

$$\frac{3}{4} \qquad\qquad\qquad \frac{5}{6} \qquad\qquad\qquad \frac{5}{8}$$

Now you have to find a common multiple for the 3 denominators.

4: 4, 8, 12, 16, 20, 24, 28, 32, 36
6: 6, 12, 18, 24, 30, 36, 42, 48   LCM = 24
8: 8, 16, 24, 32, 40, 48, 56, 64

Make equivalent fractions for each of the 3 fractions with the common multiple as their denominator and then see which fraction is the smallest.

$$\frac{3}{4} = \frac{18}{24} \qquad\qquad \frac{5}{6} = \frac{20}{24} \qquad\qquad \frac{5}{8} = \frac{15}{24}$$

2. Work out which fraction in each of these sets of fractions is the smallest. Find a common multiple for each of the denominators and then make equivalent fractions with the common multiple as the denominator.

   a) $\frac{1}{3}, \frac{2}{5}, \frac{3}{10}$
   b) $\frac{3}{4}, \frac{5}{6}, \frac{5}{8}$
   c) $\frac{1}{2}, \frac{7}{10}, \frac{3}{5}$
   d) $\frac{7}{12}, \frac{2}{3}, \frac{3}{4}$
   e) $\frac{1}{4}, \frac{3}{5}, \frac{3}{10}$
   f) $\frac{7}{8}, \frac{11}{12}, \frac{5}{6}$

Adding Fractions

If Helen spent $\frac{1}{5}$ of her money on sweets and used $\frac{1}{3}$ of her money to buy a book, what fraction of her money did she spend?

Remember: you can only add fractions that have the same denominator. If the fractions don't have the same denominator, you can make equivalent fractions with the same denominator and then add.

5: 5, 10, 15, 20, 25
3: 3, 6, 9, 12, 15, 18
The LCM is 15.

Now make equivalent fractions with the LCM as the denominator:

$$\frac{1}{5} = \frac{3}{15} \qquad\qquad \frac{1}{3} = \frac{5}{15}$$

Now add the 2 fractions:

$$\frac{3}{15} + \frac{5}{15} = \frac{8}{15}, \text{ so Helen spent } \frac{8}{15} \text{ of her money.}$$

1. Now try these.

a) $\frac{1}{2} + \frac{1}{7}$ b) $\frac{2}{5} + \frac{3}{10}$ c) $\frac{1}{3} + \frac{1}{4}$ d) $\frac{1}{9} + \frac{1}{6}$ e) $\frac{3}{8} + \frac{1}{6}$

f) $\frac{2}{5} + \frac{1}{4}$ g) $\frac{5}{12} + \frac{1}{3}$ h) $\frac{1}{10} + \frac{3}{4}$ i) $\frac{3}{5} + \frac{3}{10}$

Joe ran for $\frac{4}{5}$ of a kilometre and then walked a further $\frac{2}{5}$ of a kilometre. How far did he go altogether?

$$\frac{4}{5} + \frac{2}{5} = \frac{6}{5}$$

If your answer is an improper fraction, what can you do with it? Now what would your answer be?

2. Add these fractions and if your answer is an improper fraction, change it to a mixed number.

a) $\frac{2}{3} + \frac{3}{4}$ b) $\frac{3}{5} + \frac{3}{4}$ c) $\frac{5}{6} + \frac{3}{4}$ d) $\frac{5}{8} + \frac{2}{3}$ e) $\frac{7}{9} + \frac{5}{6}$

f) $\frac{3}{8} + \frac{5}{6}$ g) $\frac{4}{5} + \frac{7}{10}$ h) $\frac{3}{8} + \frac{7}{10}$ i) $\frac{7}{8} + \frac{7}{12}$

3. A mad scientist mixed $\frac{4}{5}$ of a litre of acid with $\frac{5}{8}$ of a litre of liquid explosive in a container to see what would happen. What was the total volume of liquid in the container before it exploded?

4. Paul used $\frac{2}{5}$ of a tin of paint to paint his hall. He used $\frac{1}{4}$ of the tin to paint the bathroom and $\frac{3}{10}$ of the tin to paint his bedroom. What fraction of the paint did he use altogether?

(Find the LCM of the 3 denominators.)

5. Now try these.

a) $\frac{1}{3} + \frac{1}{4} + \frac{1}{6}$ b) $\frac{1}{5} + \frac{1}{6} + \frac{1}{3}$ c) $\frac{1}{4} + \frac{3}{8} + \frac{1}{6}$ d) $\frac{3}{4} + \frac{2}{9} + \frac{5}{12}$ e) $\frac{3}{5} + \frac{5}{8} + \frac{7}{10}$

f) $\frac{1}{6} + \frac{9}{10} + \frac{7}{12}$ g) $\frac{1}{8} + \frac{1}{12} + \frac{1}{6}$ h) $\frac{2}{3} + \frac{3}{4} + \frac{5}{6}$ i) $\frac{4}{5} + \frac{2}{3} + \frac{5}{6}$

Subtracting Fractions

If there was $\frac{5}{6}$ of a litre of orange in a bottle and Lisa drank $\frac{1}{4}$ of a litre, how much orange would be left in the bottle?

The LCM of 6 and 4 is 12, so:

$$\frac{5}{6} = \frac{10}{12} \qquad \text{and} \qquad \frac{1}{4} = \frac{3}{12}$$
$$\frac{10}{12} - \frac{3}{12} = \frac{7}{12}$$

So there is $\frac{7}{12}$ of the orange left in the bottle.

1. Now try these.

a) $\frac{7}{8} - \frac{3}{4}$ b) $\frac{9}{10} - \frac{2}{3}$ c) $\frac{5}{6} - \frac{2}{9}$

d) $\frac{11}{12} - \frac{3}{8}$ e) $\frac{8}{9} - \frac{5}{6}$ f) $\frac{3}{5} - \frac{1}{4}$

g) $\frac{3}{4} - \frac{3}{10}$ h) $\frac{7}{8} - \frac{5}{6}$ i) $\frac{2}{3} - \frac{4}{7}$

2. Laura's hair was $\frac{3}{5}$m long. If the hairdresser cut $\frac{1}{8}$m off, how long was Laura's hair then?

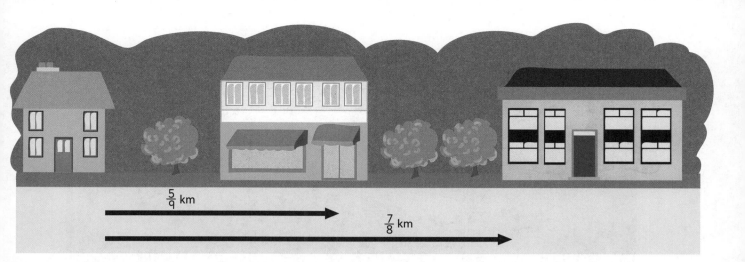

$\frac{5}{9}$ km

$\frac{7}{8}$ km

3. Bob's house is $\frac{7}{8}$km from the school. If walks $\frac{5}{9}$km to the shop on the way to school, how much further does he have to walk to get to school?

4. How much heavier than $\frac{2}{3}$kg is $\frac{9}{10}$kg?

Adding Mixed Numbers

Sophie collected $1\frac{1}{5}$kg of leaves and Eileen collected $1\frac{1}{3}$kg of leaves. What was the total weight of the leaves collected?

You have 2 choices as to how to add the mixed numbers:

Add them as mixed numbers.

$1\frac{1}{5} + 1\frac{1}{3}$

$1\frac{3}{15} + 1\frac{5}{15} = 2\frac{8}{15}$

Add them as improper fractions.

$\frac{6}{5} + \frac{4}{3}$

$\frac{18}{15} + \frac{20}{15} = \frac{38}{15} = 2\frac{8}{15}$

Which way do you prefer? Why?
Do you see any advantages of doing it one way rather than the other?
Are there any possible difficulties with either method?
What if the fractions had been $9\frac{4}{5}$ and $\frac{2}{3}$? Would there have been any problems?
Check it out both ways and see for yourself.

1. Now try these whichever way you prefer.

a) $2\frac{1}{4} + 1\frac{1}{6}$ b) $1\frac{2}{9} + 3\frac{3}{4}$ c) $2\frac{2}{5} + 3\frac{3}{10}$ d) $4\frac{1}{2} + 3\frac{5}{8}$ e) $3\frac{5}{9} + 2\frac{5}{6}$

f) $1\frac{7}{10} + 6\frac{2}{3}$ g) $9\frac{3}{7} + 2\frac{2}{3}$ h) $3\frac{7}{8} + 5\frac{4}{9}$ i) $8\frac{3}{4} + 5\frac{2}{5}$

2. The World Paper Clip Blowing Championships were held recently. In the competition, contestants were required to blow a paper clip along a polished wooden floor. Each contestant was given 3 turns to blow their paper clip and the distance the paper clip moved each time was recorded. The person who blew their paper clip the furthest when the 3 turns were added together was the winner. Can you work out who the winner was?

Contestant	Round 1	Round 2	Round 3	Total
Bob Bellows	$1\frac{1}{3}$m	$1\frac{2}{5}$m	$1\frac{5}{6}$m	?
Gail Forsyth	$1\frac{1}{2}$m	$1\frac{3}{4}$m	$1\frac{1}{6}$m	?
Don Puffin	$2\frac{1}{10}$m	$1\frac{1}{4}$m	$1\frac{1}{5}$m	?
Wendy Knight	$1\frac{8}{9}$m	$1\frac{3}{4}$m	$1\frac{5}{12}$m	?
C. Breeze	$1\frac{3}{8}$m	$1\frac{3}{10}$m	$1\frac{3}{5}$m	?

Subtracting Mixed Numbers

Sid bought a pet snake that was $1\frac{1}{2}$m long, but 2 months later it was $1\frac{4}{5}$m long. How much had the snake grown?

Again, you have 2 choices:

$1\frac{4}{5} - 1\frac{1}{2}$ $\frac{9}{5} - \frac{3}{2}$

$1\frac{8}{10} - 1\frac{5}{10}$ $\frac{18}{10} - \frac{15}{10}$

$\frac{3}{10}$ $\frac{3}{10}$

So Sid's snake grew $\frac{3}{10}$m.

1. Work these out whichever way you prefer.

  a) $1\frac{9}{10} - 1\frac{2}{3}$ b) $2\frac{3}{4} - 1\frac{1}{6}$ c) $3\frac{5}{6} - 1\frac{3}{8}$

  d) $5\frac{4}{5} - 2\frac{2}{3}$ e) $4\frac{8}{9} - 3\frac{5}{6}$ f) $8\frac{1}{5} - 4\frac{1}{8}$

  g) $4\frac{7}{12} - 2\frac{1}{4}$ h) $7\frac{5}{6} - 5\frac{2}{3}$ i) $9\frac{1}{6} - 2\frac{1}{9}$

By how much is Tall Tom taller than Tallish Ted?

Tom = $2\frac{1}{4}$m   Ted = $1\frac{5}{8}$m

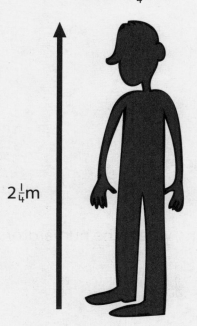
$2\frac{1}{4}$m

$1\frac{5}{8}$m

Tallish Tom   Tallish Ted

If you subtract them as mixed numbers, what is the problem?

$$2\frac{1}{4} - 1\frac{5}{8}$$
$$2\frac{2}{8} - 1\frac{5}{8}$$

But you can't subtract $\frac{5}{8}$ from $\frac{2}{8}$, so you need to borrow more $\frac{1}{8}$s from the 2 units.

$$1 \text{ unit} = \frac{8}{8}$$
$$\text{So } 2\frac{2}{8} = 1\frac{10}{8}$$
$$1\frac{10}{8} - 1\frac{5}{8} = \frac{5}{8}$$

So Tall Tom is $\frac{5}{8}$m taller than Tallish Ted.

---

2. Now subtract these as mixed numbers. Don't forget to borrow from your units.

  a) $2\frac{1}{4} - 1\frac{1}{3}$ b) $3\frac{1}{9} - 1\frac{1}{6}$ c) $4\frac{1}{5} - 2\frac{1}{4}$

  d) $9\frac{2}{5} - 3\frac{5}{6}$ e) $5\frac{3}{8} - 2\frac{2}{3}$ f) $6\frac{3}{10} - 4\frac{3}{4}$

3. Donal had an unusually long piece of liquorice, which he measured as $1\frac{1}{6}$m. If he ate a piece $\frac{5}{9}$m long, what length of liquorice was left?

4. Amy bought a bag of cement that was $9\frac{1}{2}$kg, but she didn't realise that there was a small hole in the bag. By the time she had carried it home, it weighed only $6\frac{6}{7}$kg. What was the weight of the cement that had fallen out?

Homework

1. Write equivalent fractions for each of these fractions.

    a) $\frac{1}{8}$ b) $\frac{2}{3}$ c) $\frac{4}{5}$ d) $\frac{5}{9}$ e) $\frac{7}{10}$ f) $\frac{11}{12}$

2. Now find equivalent fractions for these fractions, where the numerators and denominators are smaller.

    a) $\frac{5}{10}$ b) $\frac{9}{12}$ c) $\frac{12}{18}$ d) $\frac{9}{24}$ e) $\frac{27}{90}$ f) $\frac{40}{48}$

3. Now fill in the missing numerators/denominators to make the fractions equivalent.

    a) $\frac{1}{4} = \frac{}{36}$ b) $\frac{3}{5} = \frac{21}{}$ c) $\frac{4}{} = \frac{28}{49}$ d) $\frac{}{8} = \frac{35}{56}$ e) $\frac{2}{9} = \frac{14}{}$

    f) $\frac{9}{} = \frac{45}{50}$ g) $\frac{6}{7} = \frac{54}{}$ h) $\frac{11}{} = \frac{88}{96}$ i) $\frac{4}{5} = \frac{}{60}$ j) $\frac{8}{9} = \frac{64}{}$

4. Now change these mixed numbers into improper fractions the quick way.

    a) $1\frac{5}{6} = \frac{}{6}$ b) $2\frac{3}{4} = \frac{}{4}$ c) $3\frac{1}{5} = \frac{}{5}$ d) $2\frac{4}{9} = \frac{}{9}$ e) $4\frac{3}{8} = \frac{}{8}$

    f) $5\frac{6}{7} = \frac{}{7}$ g) $6\frac{9}{10} = \frac{}{10}$ h) $4\frac{5}{12} = \frac{}{12}$ i) $7\frac{3}{11} = \frac{}{11}$

5. Change these improper fractions into mixed numbers the quick way.

    a) $\frac{29}{4}$ b) $\frac{41}{6}$ c) $\frac{53}{8}$ d) $\frac{93}{10}$ e) $\frac{79}{12}$

    f) $\frac{26}{3}$ g) $\frac{48}{5}$ h) $\frac{59}{7}$ i) $\frac{85}{9}$ j) $\frac{95}{11}$

6. Work out which fraction in each of these pairs of fractions is bigger. Change the pairs of fractions so that they have the same denominators to help you.

    a) $\frac{1}{2}$ and $\frac{5}{9}$ b) $\frac{3}{5}$ and $\frac{2}{3}$ c) $\frac{3}{4}$ and $\frac{5}{6}$

    d) $\frac{5}{6}$ and $\frac{7}{8}$ e) $\frac{2}{5}$ and $\frac{3}{8}$ f) $\frac{5}{8}$ and $\frac{7}{12}$

7. Work out which fraction in each of these sets of fractions is the smallest. Find a common multiple for each of the denominators and then make equivalent fractions with the common multiple as the denominator.

a) $\frac{1}{2}, \frac{1}{3}, \frac{1}{4}$ b) $\frac{3}{4}, \frac{2}{3}, \frac{5}{6}$ c) $\frac{3}{4}, \frac{4}{5}, \frac{7}{10}$ d) $\frac{5}{12}, \frac{5}{6}, \frac{3}{4}$ e) $\frac{2}{3}, \frac{5}{6}, \frac{7}{9}$ f) $\frac{3}{8}, \frac{7}{12}, \frac{5}{6}$

8. Add these fractions. If your answer is an improper fraction, then change it to a mixed number.

a) $\frac{1}{2} + \frac{5}{6}$ b) $\frac{2}{3} + \frac{7}{9}$ c) $\frac{1}{6} + \frac{8}{9}$ d) $\frac{3}{8} + \frac{2}{3}$ e) $\frac{5}{8} + \frac{5}{12}$ f) $\frac{7}{8} + \frac{3}{4}$

9. Now try these.

a) $\frac{5}{6} - \frac{1}{4}$ b) $\frac{7}{8} - \frac{2}{3}$ c) $\frac{4}{5} - \frac{7}{10}$ d) $\frac{8}{9} - \frac{1}{6}$ e) $\frac{7}{12} - \frac{3}{8}$ f) $\frac{4}{5} - \frac{3}{4}$

10. Now try these whichever way you prefer.

a) $2\frac{1}{3} + 1\frac{1}{6}$ b) $1\frac{3}{4} + 4\frac{3}{8}$ c) $3\frac{4}{5} + 1\frac{9}{10}$ d) $5\frac{5}{6} + 2\frac{3}{4}$ e) $3\frac{3}{4} + 2\frac{2}{3}$ f) $4\frac{7}{8} + 3\frac{1}{6}$

11. Now subtract these as mixed numbers. Don't forget to borrow from your units if you need to.

a) $3\frac{1}{2} - 1\frac{3}{8}$ b) $4\frac{1}{6} - 2\frac{2}{3}$ c) $5\frac{1}{5} - 1\frac{7}{10}$ d) $6\frac{3}{4} - 4\frac{5}{6}$ e) $7\frac{3}{5} - 2\frac{3}{4}$ f) $6\frac{8}{9} - 4\frac{5}{6}$

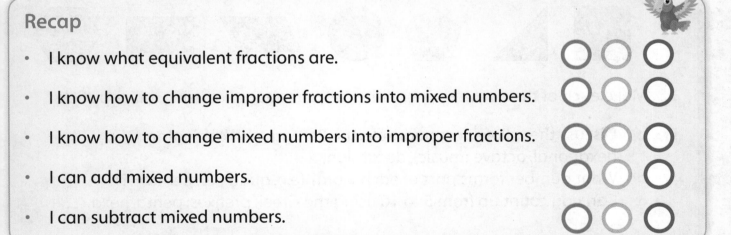

Recap

- I know what equivalent fractions are. ○ ○ ○

- I know how to change improper fractions into mixed numbers. ○ ○ ○

- I know how to change mixed numbers into improper fractions. ○ ○ ○

- I can add mixed numbers. ○ ○ ○

- I can subtract mixed numbers. ○ ○ ○

Talk About

Have a look around your classroom. Name and find examples of as many 2-D shapes as possible.

What shape is the whiteboard, pane of glass in the window and your tabletop?

What is the most common 2-D shape in the classroom?

Why do you think this is so?

 Remember: two-dimensional (2-D) shapes are so called because they have only 2 dimensions: length and width.

Properties of 2-D Shapes

1. Identify these 2-D shapes and describe the shapes using the following headings: number of lines, number of angles, parallel lines, equal length, perpendicular lines, right angles, acute angles, obtuse angles.

2. Make each of the above shapes either on a geoboard or using lollipop sticks.

3. a) Discuss the following: quadruple, the Pentagon (Washington, DC), hexagonal, octave (music), decathlon.
   b) What number forms part of each word? (e.g. quad = 4, penta = ?)
   c) Can you count up from 5 to 10 using the Greek prefixes: penta, hexa, …

 Remember: 2-D shapes that have the same number of sides and angles are called **polygons**.

A **regular polygon** is a polygon with sides of the same length, and with angles that are all the same.

Strand: Shape and Space
Curriculum Objectives:
Make informal deductions about 2-D shapes and their properties;
use angle and line properties to classify and describe triangles.
construct triangles from given sides or angles;
use 2-D shapes and properties to solve problems.

4. Name and draw 5 regular polygons.

5. a) Match the triangle to its description.

   3 equal sides   2 equal sides   No equal sides
   3 equal angles of 60°   2 equal angles   No equal angles

   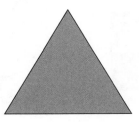

   b) Now match the triangle to its correct name.

      equilateral triangle   isosceles triangle   scalene triangle

6. What shape am I?
   a) I have 6 sides.
   b) I have as many sides as an ant has legs.
   c) I have 4 sides of equal length.
   d) I have 3 sides, none of which are the same length.
   e) I have as many sides as you have toes on one foot.
   f) I have 4 sides. Only one pair of sides are parallel.
   g) Draw an example of each of the above shapes.

Puzzler

Inspector Pentagon walked into the drawing room of Shape Hall to find the maid, Ms Circle, lying dead on the floor. All of the suspects for the murder were present: Lord Rectangle, Lady Rhombus, Sir Square, Prince Parallelogram and media mogul Terence Triangle. Inspector Pentagon took one look around the room and announced that he knew who was guilty of the terrible crime. 'The person who is responsible for this infamous act has 4 sides,' he announced. Terence Triangle heaved a sigh of relief. The inspector directed the 2 policemen who were with him to arrest the person whose opposite sides were equal, whose opposite sides were parallel, who had 4 right angles and who was a regular kind of a chap. The policemen scratched their heads and looked at each other in bewilderment. They did not know who to arrest. Can you follow all of the clues and help them to identify the guilty person?

A **quadrilateral** is a 4-sided polygon. The sum of the angles of a quadrilateral is 360°.

7. Which of these shapes are quadrilaterals?

a)

b)

c) 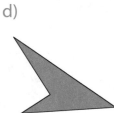 d)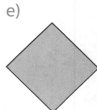

e)

8. Complete the table.

Shape	Equal sides	Equal angles	Pairs of parallel lines
Square			
Rhombus			
Isosceles triangle			
Rectangle			
Equilateral triangle			
Trapezium			

 Remember: the sum of the angles of a triangle = 180°.

9. Find the missing angle in each of these.

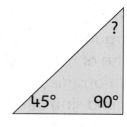

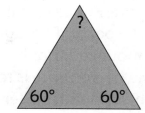

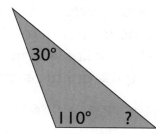

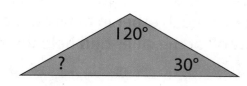

To do the following activities, you will need a protractor like this one.

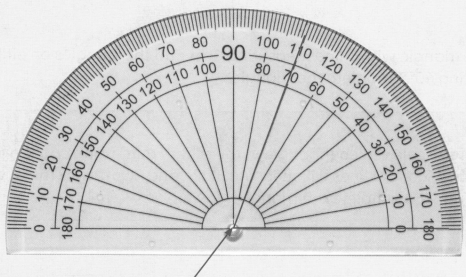

To measure an angle, place the centre point of the protractor on the point where the 2 lines meet.

Keeping the centre point on this point, twist the protractor until the 0° line is lined up along 1 of the lines making the angle.

Finally, read where the second line is pointing to on the protractor (in this case, 70, so the angle is 70°).

Constructing a Triangle

1. a) Can you finish drawing this triangle?
    b) What is the length of the third side of this triangle?
    c) What do the other angles measure?
    d) Name this type of triangle.

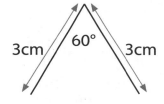

2. Complete the construction of each of these triangles on a piece of paper.

    a) 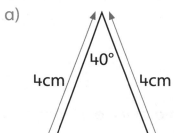   b) 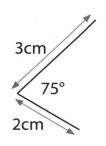   c)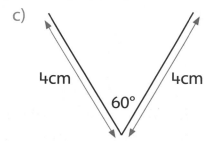

3. Measure and record the third side and the 2 missing angles on each of the triangles from question 2.

4. Construct a triangle with 1 line measuring 5cm and the 2 angles on this line measuring 100° and 35°. Measure the remaining sides and angle and complete the triangle.

5. Construct a triangle with an angle of 70° between 2 equal lines measuring 6.5cm. Find the length of the third side and the 2 remaining angles. What type of triangle is this?

6. Construct a triangle with 1 line measuring 6cm and the 2 angles on either end of this line measuring 60°. Complete the triangle.

Task:
Construct a large-scale scalene triangle in the school yard using chalk, a protractor and a metre stick. 2 of the lines will measure 55cm and 90cm, with the angle between them measuring 50°. Complete the triangle.

Tessellating Shapes

Have a look at this photograph of the Giant's Causeway in Co. Antrim. Do you notice any tessellating shape?

This is a natural example of a tessellation. Can you think of any more examples?

 Remember: tessellation, or **tiling**, means arranging shapes in a repeated pattern so as to leave no spaces.

1. The diagram shows an example of squares tessellating.

Draw an example of each of the following 2-D shapes on a piece of paper and decide if the shapes tessellate or not.
   a) circle
   b) rectangle
   c) trapezium
   d) rhombus
   e) pentagon
   f) triangle
   g) Colour in your tessellations to make interesting patterns.

2. Design your own tessellating patttern.

Homework

1. Do you know your shapes? Fill in the table.

Shape	Number of sides	Number of angles	Are all sides equal?	Are opposite sides equal?	Number of right angles
Rectangle					
Isosceles triangle					
Hexagon					
Circle					
Square					
Pentagon					
Trapezium					
Rhombus					
Parallelogram					

2. What is the size of the missing angle in each of these triangles?

   a) 38°, 95°, ?
   b) 108°, 23°, ?
   c) 78°, 83°, ?
   d) 117°, 45°, ?
   e) 64°, 98°, ?
   f) 17°, 59°, ?

3. Construct a triangle with 1 line measuring 8cm and the 2 angles on either end of this line measuring 43° and 75°. Complete the triangle.

4. Look around your home and see if you can find an example of tessellation.
   (Hint: you might have some success in the kitchen or in the bathroom.)

5. Design a tessellating pattern of your own and colour it in.

Recap

- I can identify 2-D shapes. ○ ○ ○

- I can construct triangles. ○ ○ ○

- I know what tessellation means. ○ ○ ○

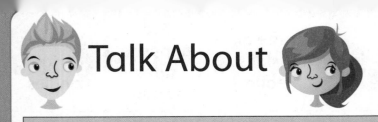

Talk About

Task:
Find out the difference between the numbers on the registration plates of the cars of any 2 teachers in your school. Ignore the year and county of origin (e.g. if the teacher's registration plate reads 00 MH 23592, just focus on the 23592). Show only your answer to the people near you and see if they can guess which 2 teachers you chose.

1. Round these numbers up or down to the nearest 10.
    a) 38
    b) 71
    c) 104
    d) 26
    e) 89
    f) 123
    g) 177
    h) 214
    i) 292
    j) 337
    k) 406
    l) 995

    As you know, when you want to estimate the answers to multiplication questions, rounding up or down is very helpful.

Estimating and Calculating Products

2. Estimate the total contents of the following groceries by rounding up or down to the nearest 10.
    a) There are 79 peas in a tin. How many peas are there in 11 tins?
    b) There are 8 squares in a bar of chocolate. How many squares are there in 27 bars?
    c) There are 12 eggs in a dozen. How many eggs are there in 32 dozen?
    d) There are 17 flowers in a bouquet of flowers. How many flowers are there in 41 bouquets?
    e) There are 52 cards in a deck of cards. How many cards are there in 23 decks?
    f) There are 59 crisps in a packet of crisps. How many crisps are there in 44 packets?

Strand: Number
Curriculum Objectives:
Estimate and calculate products and quotients;
divide a 4-digit number by a 2-digit number without and with a calculator

If 1 of the numbers in the multiplication question is over 100, then you have 2 choices: you can round the number to the nearest hundred or you can round it to the nearest ten.

$$183 \times 28 =$$

Round to the nearest hundred:

$$\begin{array}{r} 200 \\ \times \quad 30 \\ \hline 600 \end{array}$$

Round to the nearest 10:

$$\begin{array}{r} 180 \\ \times \quad 30 \\ \hline 5400 \end{array}$$

Which estimate will be more accurate? Why?

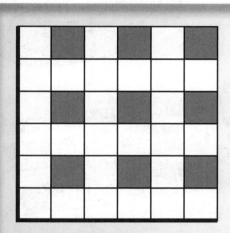

Puzzler

A kitchen floor is to be tiled in the pattern shown on the left:

If the kitchen floor measures 13 tiles × 21 tiles, how many white tiles will be needed?

1. Estimate the answers to these by rounding to either the nearest 100 or 10. Then work out the answers to see how accurate your estimates are.

    a) 98 × 32
    b) 124 × 37
    c) 191 × 42
    d) 213 × 58
    e) 257 × 51
    f) 288 × 46
    g) 149 × 72
    h) 422 × 60
    i) 466 × 89

    How many choices would you have for rounding up or down if 1 of the numbers in the multiplication is over 1000?

2. Write down the different possible estimates for this: 1231 × 37.

3. Now estimate the answers to these and then work out the answers to see how accurate each estimate is.

    a) 1076 × 29
    b) 982 × 43
    c) 1617 × 32
    d) 2204 × 46
    e) 2759 × 51
    f) 3186 × 67

4. Use your calculator to work out the answers to these.

a) 2154
× 35
___

b) 1392
× 27
___

c) 2438
× 18
___

d) 4582
× 43
___

e) 3545
× 24
___

f) 1947
× 48
___

g) 2280
× 33
___

h) 8116
× 45
___

i) 5076
× 52
___

j) 3461
× 68
___

k) 7508
× 84
___

l) 6732
× 76
___

5. A shop sold 1934 baseball caps at €25 each. How much money did the shop take in for the baseball caps?

6. If there are 2566 holes in a string vest, how many holes are there in 48 string vests?

7. An army of 3275 aliens invaded Earth. Each of the aliens had 38 eyes. How many eyes did the army of aliens have altogether?

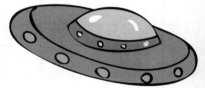

8. If a librarian can fit 637 books on a shelf, how many books could the librarian fit on 54 shelves?

9. The group Supertonic released their new album last week. The record company sent 4724 copies of the CD to each of 86 different record shops. At the end of the week all of the record shops had sold out. How many copies of the CD were sold?

Estimating and Calculating Quotients

If 6 eggs make up a full tray, how many trays of eggs can be filled with 174 eggs?

You have 2 choices.

You can keep subtracting 6 from 174 until there aren't enough eggs left to subtract 6. The number of times you were able to subtract will tell you how many trays could be filled.

$$
\begin{array}{r}
174 \\
- 6 \\
\hline
168 \\
- 6 \\
\hline
\end{array}
$$

Or you can divide 6 into 174 to see how many trays can be filled and if there are any eggs left over.

$$6 \overline{\smash{)}174}$$

1. Work out the answers to these.
   a) If there are 8 apples in a bag, how many bags can be filled with 136 apples?
   b) If there are 4 markers in a packet, how many packets can be filled with 237 markers?
   c) If there are 11 strawberries in a punnet, how many punnets can be filled with 396 strawberries?
   d) If there are 7 doughnuts in a box, how many boxes can be filled with 483 doughnuts?
   e) If there are 9 prawn crackers in a basket, how many baskets can be filled with 1265 prawn crackers?
   f) If there are 5 cakes in a bag, how many bags can be filled with 2478 cakes?

2. Now try these.
   a) 1365 ÷ 7
   b) 2908 ÷ 6
   c) 2535 ÷ 5
   d) 4752 ÷ 11
   e) 5713 ÷ 9
   f) 6597 ÷ 3
   g) 8117 ÷ 12
   h) 9590 ÷ 10
   i) 7152 ÷ 8

3. A car transporter can carry up 12 cars at one time (6 up and 6 down). How many car transporters would be needed to carry 2712 cars?

A school with 672 pupils was divided into classes of 28. Estimate how many classes were in the school.

$$692 ÷ 28$$

Round both numbers to the nearest 10:

$$690 ÷ 30 = 23$$

So your estimate would be 23.

4. Estimate the answers to these division questions by rounding up or down to the nearest 10.
   a) 238 ÷ 19
   b) 273 ÷ 28
   c) 318 ÷ 42
   d) 279 ÷ 68
   e) 346 ÷ 52
   f) 419 ÷ 63
   g) 541 ÷ 87
   h) 637 ÷ 81
   i) 393 ÷ 28

Remember: you can work out division by changing it to multiplication.

While training for a race, an athlete ran exactly the same distance every day for 2 weeks. If she ran a total distance of 112km, what distance did she run each day?

$$112 \div 14$$

But this can also be written as:

$$14 \times ? = 112$$

Now make an estimate as to what the missing number is, then multiply and see how close your answer is to 112. If your answer is too small, try a bigger number. If it's too big, try a smaller number.

5. Rewrite these division questions as multiplication and then work out the missing numbers. Use a rough work column to test your estimates.

   a) $114 \div 19$ b) $168 \div 24$ c) $152 \div 19$

   d) $112 \div 28$ e) $280 \div 35$ f) $138 \div 46$

Sometimes the numbers will not divide in evenly.

John has been saving money in his piggy bank for months. Now he wants to put it into his bank account to keep it safe. The bank will only accept coins in their proper bags. To fill a bank bag, he needs 25 €1 coins. John has 178 €1 coins. How many bags can he fill?

$$178 \div 25 = ? \text{ is the same as } 25 \times ? = 178$$

Try different numbers to see how close you can get to 175 without going over it.

How would you work out the remainder?

$$
\begin{array}{r}
7 \\
25\,\overline{)\,178} \\
-\,175 \\
\hline
\text{R3}
\end{array}
\qquad
\begin{array}{r}
25 \\
\times\ \ 7 \\
\hline
175
\end{array}
$$

This means that John can fill 7 bags and that he will have 3 €1 coins left over.

6. Now try these. Don't forget the remainders.

   a) $173 \div 26$ b) $145 \div 38$ c) $201 \div 33$

   d) $428 \div 59$ e) $326 \div 47$ f) $219 \div 55$

Sometimes when you divide, you will get tens and units in the answer.

Frank invited 18 people to his birthday party and he made 306 fairy cakes. Can you help him work out how many cakes each person (including himself) should get?

```
     017
18 | 306
   - 180
    126
   - 126
      0
```

We see that 18 goes into 30 once, but that 1 is in the tens column, so it's really 18 × 10. Therefore, we subtract 180 to get our first remainder.

Now we can estimate how many times 18 will go into 126 so that we can get an answer in the units column and see if there is a remainder. 18 × 7 = 126, so 7 is the answer in the units column and there is no remainder.

So each person will get 17 cakes.

7. Now try these.

a) 375 ÷ 25
b) 416 ÷ 16
c) 704 ÷ 22
d) 784 ÷ 28
e) 850 ÷ 34
f) 774 ÷ 43

8. Debbie broke the world record for fitting 442 jelly babies into her mouth at the same time. If this was a total of 26 packets of jelly babies, how many were in each packet?

9. How many times can I take €29 away from €827? How many euro will be left over?

10. If Tommy the Tie Collector went into a shop and bought 38 ties at a total cost of €646, how much did each tie cost?

11. A path was 1134cm long. How many jumps of 54cm did it take a grasshopper to travel along the length of the path?

It took Bill 14 years to collect 1848 paper hats. If he collected the same number of hats every year, how many did he collect each year?

```
       1
14 | 1848
```

14 goes into 18 once, but this answer is in the hundreds column so it's really 14 × 100 = 1400.

```
        132
    ┌────────
14 │ 1848
    − 1400
    ────────
      448
    − 420
    ────────
       28
     − 28
    ────────
        0
```

Now we can get an answer in the tens column by estimating how many times 14 goes into 44.

$14 × 3 = 42$, so we can put 3 in the tens column. This is really $14 × 30 = 420$, so we subtract 420.

Now we can get an answer in the units column by estimating how many times 14 goes into 28. $14 × 2 = 28$, so 2 is the answer in the units column and there is no remainder.

So he collected 132 hats every year.

12. Try these ones yourself.

a) $1742 ÷ 13$ b) $2280 ÷ 15$ c) $2394 ÷ 19$

d) $4945 ÷ 23$ e) $4941 ÷ 27$ f) $4774 ÷ 31$

g) $5216 ÷ 16$ h) $6350 ÷ 25$ i) $6052 ÷ 34$

13. A total of 2176 passengers travelled on 17 flights to Portugal. If all of the flights were full, how many people were on each plane?

14. Divide a prize of €4550 evenly among 26 people.

Homework

1. Estimate the answers to these and then work out the answers to see how accurate each estimate is.

a) $1095 × 31$ b) $996 × 38$ c) $1495 × 29$

d) $2309 × 48$ e) $3898 × 52$ f) $3201 × 78$

2. Now try these. Check your answers with a calculator.

a) 1436	b) 3124	c) 3682	d) 1769	e) 2638	f) 4108
× 28	× 32	× 19	× 24	× 35	× 37

g) 5093	h) 7247	i) 3945	j) 1864	k) 4256	l) 3187
× 16	× 43	× 48	× 65	× 59	× 74

3. Now try these.

a) $6769 ÷ 7$ b) $3942 ÷ 9$ c) $4232 ÷ 8$

d) $5016 ÷ 6$ e) $3084 ÷ 12$ f) $7495 ÷ 5$

4. Estimate the answers to these division questions by rounding up or down to the nearest 10.
   a) 262 ÷ 18
   b) 218 ÷ 21
   c) 278 ÷ 38
   d) 358 ÷ 59
   e) 322 ÷ 81
   f) 489 ÷ 73

5. Rewrite these division questions as multiplication and then work out the missing numbers. Use a rough work column to test your estimates.
   a) 126 ÷ 18
   b) 161 ÷ 23
   c) 216 ÷ 27
   d) 153 ÷ 17
   e) 174 ÷ 29
   f) 304 ÷ 38

6. Now try these.
   a) 408 ÷ 24
   b) 494 ÷ 19
   c) 504 ÷ 28
   d) 988 ÷ 26
   e) 945 ÷ 35
   f) 1092 ÷ 42

7. Try these too.
   a) 1890 ÷ 14
   b) 2544 ÷ 16
   c) 5103 ÷ 21
   d) 4200 ÷ 25
   e) 3973 ÷ 29
   f) 7412 ÷ 34

8. Rock band Numbskull sold out their concert venue for 16 consecutive nights. If the venue holds 4986, how many people attended their concerts?

9. If there are 24 toilet rolls in every box, how many boxes can be filled from 1740 rolls and how many will be left over?

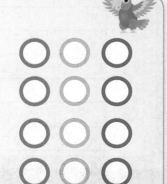

Recap

- I can estimate products.
- I can calculate products.
- I can estimate quotients.
- I can calculate quotients.

Talk About

Think About

What are the chances of you guessing the month in which your teacher's birthday falls?

There is a ____ in ____ chance of guessing correctly.

What would the chances be if you knew that s/he was born in winter?
What about if s/he was were born in a month that has the letter *m* in it?
Now make up your own possibilities and try them out on your friends.

Exploring Outcomes of Random Processes

1. Roll 2 dice. Add the numbers shown on the dice.
   Now roll the dice again. Find the total again. Did you get the same answer?
   Try it a few more times and keep a record of the totals of the numbers.
   Now compare your results with those of the people around you.
   How many possible results do you think there are?
   Fill in this table with all of the possible outcomes. The first few have been done for you.

Total	Combinations of dice that give this total
2	1 + 1
3	2 + 1
4	1 + 3, 2 + 2

a) How many combinations of results are there?
b) Which totals are you most likely to get?
c) Which totals are you least likely to get?
d) Check your own results and see which totals came up most frequently.
e) What are the chances of rolling a 12?
f) What are the chances of rolling a 5?
g) What are the chances of rolling a 7?

2. On separate pieces of paper/card, write each of the single-digit odd numbers.

Now place each of the pieces of paper/card into a bag or a box and pick out 2 numbers without looking. Record the result.
Put the numbers back in the bag and choose again. Did you get a different result? Record your answer again.
Choose 10 times. How many different results did you get?
Did the person beside you get any results that you didn't get?

a) Write down all the possible outcomes there are.
b) How many possible outcomes did you find?
c) What are the chances of the numbers selected being 1 and 9?
d) What are the chances of 1 of the numbers chosen being a 3?
   (There is a ____ in ____ of 1 of the numbers chosen being a 3.)
e) What are the chances of 1 of the numbers chosen being a 6?
   (There is a ____ in ____ of one of the numbers chosen being a 6.)

Estimating the Likelihood of Certain Outcomes

1. This is a keypad on a locked door. To unlock the door you have to press 2 of the numbers in the right order. You can repeat the same number twice.
   a) How many possible combinations are there? List them out.
   b) What are the chances of you getting the right combination?
   c) What are the chances of you getting 1 of the numbers right?
   d) If you were not allowed to repeat any of the numbers, how many possible outcomes would there be?

2. Complete these sentences so that they are true.

   a) When you toss a coin there are ____ possible outcomes.

   b) There is a ____ in ____ chance of tossing a coin and getting a tail.

   c) As a fraction, there is a ____ / ____ chance of tossing a tail.

   d) We can also write this fraction as a percentage: there is a ____% chance of tossing a tail.

3. Put 2 red cubes and 3 blue cubes into a bag. Pick out 1 cube and record what colour it is. Replace it in the bag and choose again. Choose 20 times. Record the result each time.

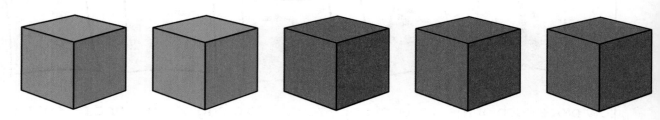

   a) Which colour is more likely to be picked?

   b) What are the chances of picking a red cube?

   c) Write this as a fraction and then work out what percentage chance it represents.

   d) What are the chances of picking a blue cube?

   e) Write this as a fraction and then work out what percentage chance it represents.

   f) Based on these percentages, how many times might you expect to get a red cube if you chose 50 times?

   g) How many times might you expect to get a blue cube if you chose 80 times?

   h) If you put an extra blue cube into the bag, what would the chances now be of picking a blue cube, and what would be the chances be of picking a red cube?

   i) Now write these chances as fractions.

   j) Look at the fractions closely. Can they be written in any other way?

   k) Now write them as percentages.

4. Write the chances of these events happening as a fraction and as a percentage.

   a) Rolling a die and getting an odd number

   b) Rolling a die and getting a multiple of 3

   c) Picking a diamond card from a deck of cards

   d) Being born in a month whose name starts with a J

   e) Being born in a month whose name has an A in it

   f) Being born in a month whose name has an R in it

Looking at Frequency Tables

1. Put 1 green marble, 1 blue marble and 2 red marbles into a bag. Pick 1 marble out and record the result. Pick 10 times. Keep a record of the outcomes. Put your results together with the results of 9 other people so that you can see the results of 100 picks. Put your answers in a frequency table like this one.

Colour	Number of times picked (frequency)
Green	
Blue	
Red	

Based on your results, you would say:

a) The chances of picking a green marble $= \frac{}{100} =$ ____%

b) The chances of picking a blue marble $= \frac{}{100} =$ ____%

c) The chances of picking a red marble $= \frac{}{100} =$ ____%

d) Based on the number of marbles in the bag, is this what you would have expected? If it isn't, what would you have expected?

2. Now look at this frequency table, which shows the number of times coloured cubes were picked from a bag.

Colour	Frequency
Yellow	22
Pink	9
White	19

a) Based on the frequency with which each colour was picked, what are the percentage chances of each colour being picked?

Yellow $= \frac{22}{50} =$ ____%   Pink $= \frac{9}{50} =$ ____%   White $= \frac{19}{50} =$ ____%

b) If there are 5 cubes in the bag, how many cubes of each different colour are likely to be in the bag?

Task:
Put 8 coloured cubes into a bag. The 8 cubes should be made up of 4 different-coloured cubes. Don't let the people near you see how many of each different-coloured cube you have put into the bag. Now get the people near you to pick out cubes 60 times. Construct a frequency table to record the results. Now see if your friends can guess how many of each different-coloured cubes are in the bag.

Recap

- I can explore possible outcomes of certain processes.   ◯ ◯ ◯

- I can construct and use frequency tables.   ◯ ◯ ◯

Talk About

Joan had only $\frac{1}{3}$ of her bar of chocolate left when her best friend, Ayshea, asked if she could have some. Being a very good friend, Joan gave Ayshea half of what she had left. What fraction of the bar did she give Ayshea?

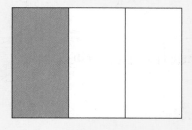

$\frac{1}{3}$

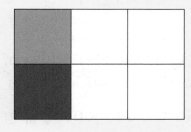

$\frac{1}{2}$ of $\frac{1}{3}$

$\frac{1}{2}$ of $\frac{1}{3}$ will be the shaded area, but what fraction does this represent?

$$\frac{1}{2} \text{ of } \frac{1}{3} = \frac{1}{6}$$

Do you see any relationship between the numerators and denominators of the 2 fractions and the numerator and denominator of the answer?

$$1 \times 1 = 1$$
$$2 \times 3 = 6$$

Let's have a look at another one and see if the pattern is the same.

Bob had only $\frac{3}{5}$ of his bar of chocolate left when his best friend, Oisín, asked if he could have some. Bob was not quite as good a friend as Joan was and he gave Oisín only one-quarter of what he had left. What fraction of the bar did he give Oisín?

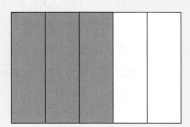

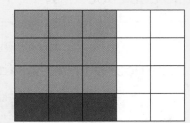

$\frac{1}{4}$ of $\frac{3}{5}$ is the shaded area, but what fraction does it represent? Is there any relationship between the numerators and denominators?

$$1 \times 3 = 3$$
$$4 \times 5 = 20$$

To find a fraction of another fraction, you just _____ the fractions.

a) subtract   b) multiply   c) eat

Multiplying Fractions by Fractions

1. Work these out. Draw the fractions to check your answers.

a) $\frac{1}{2}$ of $\frac{1}{4}$ b) $\frac{1}{3}$ of $\frac{1}{6}$ c) $\frac{1}{4}$ of $\frac{2}{3}$ d) $\frac{2}{3}$ of $\frac{3}{4}$ e) $\frac{1}{5}$ of $\frac{2}{5}$ f) $\frac{1}{8}$ of $\frac{1}{2}$

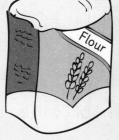

John was baking a cake. He had $\frac{2}{3}$kg of flour but he used only $\frac{1}{2}$ of it. How much flour did he use?

What is $\frac{1}{2}$ of $\frac{2}{3}$? To find out, you multiply the fractions.

$$\frac{1}{2} \times \frac{2}{3} = \frac{2}{6}$$

Look at the answer carefully. What do you notice about it? You can divide by a member of the family of 1 to get an equivalent fraction with a smaller numerator and denominator.

But which member of the family of 1 do you divide by?

$$\frac{2}{6} \div \frac{2}{2} = \frac{1}{3}$$

June was also baking a cake. She had $\frac{3}{4}$kg of flour and used $\frac{2}{3}$ of it. How much flour did she use?

$$\frac{2}{3} \text{ of } \frac{3}{4}$$
$$\frac{2}{3} \times \frac{3}{4} = \frac{6}{12}$$

But there is more than one member of the family of 1 you can divide by. What are they? Which one should you choose? Why? Talk about it with the people sitting near you.

2. Try these. Reduce your answers as far as you can by dividing by members of the family of 1.

a) $\frac{1}{2}$ of $\frac{2}{5}$ b) $\frac{1}{3}$ of $\frac{3}{4}$ c) $\frac{5}{6}$ of $\frac{1}{5}$ d) $\frac{4}{9}$ of $\frac{3}{4}$ e) $\frac{5}{8}$ of $\frac{4}{5}$

f) $\frac{7}{8} \times \frac{4}{7}$ g) $\frac{5}{12} \times \frac{3}{5}$ h) $\frac{2}{3} \times \frac{9}{10}$ i) $\frac{4}{7} \times \frac{7}{12}$ j) $\frac{9}{10} \times \frac{5}{12}$

You can save yourself the job of reducing your answer if you reduce the numerators and denominators before you multiply.

You can reduce any numerator and any denominator if there is a common factor.

$$\frac{5}{8} \times \frac{3}{10}$$

Look at the opposite numerators and denominators. Is there a common factor that will divide into both 3 and 8? Is there a common factor that will divide into both 5 and 10?

$$\frac{\overset{1}{\cancel{5}}}{8} \times \frac{3}{\underset{2}{\cancel{10}}}$$

So now
$$\frac{1}{8} \times \frac{3}{2} = \frac{3}{16}$$

3. Look for common factors of the numerators and denominators and then reduce before multiplying the fractions.

   a) $\frac{4}{5} \times \frac{7}{8}$
   b) $\frac{5}{6} \times \frac{3}{10}$
   c) $\frac{8}{9} \times \frac{3}{4}$
   d) $\frac{3}{8} \times \frac{6}{7}$
   e) $\frac{5}{9} \times \frac{6}{11}$

   f) $\frac{9}{10} \times \frac{2}{3}$
   g) $\frac{4}{7} \times \frac{7}{8}$
   h) $\frac{1}{12} \times \frac{9}{10}$
   i) $\frac{11}{12} \times \frac{8}{11}$

Dividing a Whole Number by a Fraction

Raymond decided to bring oranges for his rugby team to eat at half time. He had 5 oranges and divided them into quarters. How many quarters did he have altogether?

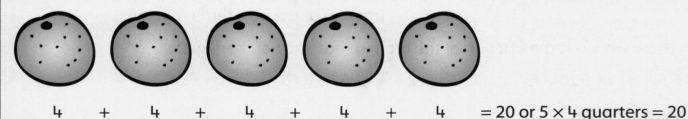

    4   +   4   +   4   +   4   +   4   = 20 or 5 × 4 quarters = 20

So there are 20 quarters in 5 oranges.

1. How many quarters are in the following?

   a) 7 oranges   b) 4 oranges   c) 11 oranges

   d) 9 oranges   e) 12 oranges   f) 18 oranges

2. a) $2 \div \frac{1}{4}$ b) $4 \div 8$ c) $15 \div \frac{1}{5}$ d) $3 \div \frac{1}{6}$

Ratios

1. Greedy Graham had 12 sweets. He was supposed to share them equally with his friend Gavin, but for every 1 sweet he gave Gavin, he took 2 for himself. How many sweets did each of them get?

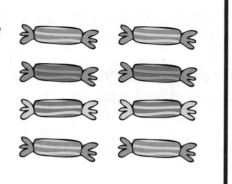

Greedy Graham divided the sweets in a ratio of 2 : 1. **Ratio** means the way in which amounts are divided.

So the sweets were divided into 3 shares and Greedy Graham got 2 of the shares and poor Gavin got only 1 share. What fraction of the sweets did each of the boys get?

Greedy Graham   Gavin

2. Before going up the hill, Jack and Jill did a spot of housework for their parents. Their mother gave them €20 for the work they had done, but because Jack was lazy and didn't do as much work as Jill, she insisted the money be divided in a ratio of 3 : 2 in favour of Jill. How much did each of them get?

First of all, work out how many shares there are altogether. (Hint: add the 2 sides of the ratio together.) This gives you the denominator of the fraction of the €20 that each gets.

Now work out the fraction of the money that each of them gets.

Jill = $\frac{3}{?}$ of €20 = €?   Jack = $\frac{2}{?}$ of €20 = €?

Puzzler

The teachers in St Patrick's NS had a Lotto syndicate. Each week Ms Flynn, Mr Murphy and Mrs Maguire put in €3 each, while Mr Skinflint, the principal, only put €1 in. One week, 5 of their numbers came up and they won €27850. The teachers who put in €3 every week felt it would be fairer if the money was divided up in accordance with the amount of money they all put in each week. Can you work out what Mr Skinflint's share of the prize was and what each of the 3 teachers received?

3. Divide these amounts of money between Tony and Adam according to the ratio indicated. Tony's share is the first number in each of the ratios.

a) Share €24 in a ratio of 3 : 1
b) Share €30 in a ratio of 2 : 3
c) Share €56 in a ratio of 4 : 3
d) Share €27 in a ratio of 2 : 1
e) Share €48 in a ratio of 3 : 5
f) Share €72 in a ratio of 5 : 4

Gemma and Sinéad won a prize in a raffle. They divided it between them so that Gemma got €40 and Sinéad got €24. What ratio did they divide the prize in?

If Gemma got €40 and Sinéad got €24, the total prize was €64. What fraction of the total prize did each get?

$$\text{Gemma} = \frac{40}{64} \qquad\qquad \text{Sinéad} = \frac{24}{64}$$

Now reduce the fractions to their lowest terms.

$$\frac{40}{64} = \frac{5}{8} \qquad\qquad\qquad \frac{24}{64} = \frac{3}{8}$$

The 2 numerators give you the ratio, so the prize was divided in a ratio of 5 : 3.

4. Work out what ratios were used to divide these prizes. Remember to add the 2 amounts to work out the total prize first.

a) Joe got €16 and Jim got €8
b) Lorraine got €24 and Simon got €16
c) Phil got €30 and Paula got €50
d) Laura got €48 and Richard got €40

Homework

1. Work these out. Draw the fractions to check your answers.

a) $\frac{1}{3}$ of $\frac{1}{5}$
b) $\frac{1}{2}$ of $\frac{2}{3}$
c) $\frac{1}{4}$ of $\frac{1}{6}$
d) $\frac{2}{3}$ of $\frac{4}{5}$
e) $\frac{3}{4}$ of $\frac{2}{5}$
f) $\frac{3}{8}$ of $\frac{1}{2}$

2. Try these. Reduce your answers as far as you can by dividing by members of the family of 1.

a) $\frac{2}{3}$ of $\frac{1}{6}$
b) $\frac{3}{4}$ of $\frac{5}{6}$
c) $\frac{1}{8}$ of $\frac{4}{5}$
d) $\frac{5}{9} \times \frac{3}{4}$
e) $\frac{7}{8} \times \frac{5}{7}$
f) $\frac{8}{9} \times \frac{6}{7}$
g) $\frac{2}{5} \times \frac{3}{8}$
h) $\frac{3}{10} \times \frac{4}{9}$
i) $\frac{3}{5} \times \frac{5}{12}$

3. Look for common factors of the numerators and denominators and then reduce before multiplying the fractions.

a) $\frac{6}{7} \times \frac{3}{4}$

b) $\frac{8}{9} \times \frac{3}{10}$

c) $\frac{5}{8} \times \frac{7}{10}$

d) $\frac{5}{6} \times \frac{9}{10}$

e) $\frac{7}{12} \times \frac{6}{7}$

f) $\frac{3}{8} \times \frac{2}{9}$

4. a) Share €126 in a ratio of 1 : 2

b) Share €164 in a ratio of 3 : 1

c) Share €245 in a ratio of 2 : 3

d) Share €413 in a ratio of 4 : 3

e) Share €342 in a ratio of 1 : 5

f) Share €608 in a ratio of 5 : 3

5. If Ronan gave 32 Stat Attack cards to his friend and kept 48 cards for himself, what ratio did he divide the cards in?

Recap

- I can multiply fractions. ○ ○ ○

- I can cancel fractions before multiplying. ○ ○ ○

- I can express 1 number as a fraction of another. ○ ○ ○

- I know what ratio means. ○ ○ ○

- I can divide amounts in accordance with a ratio. ○ ○ ○

 # Talk About

1. List as many circular objects as you can see around you.

> **Remember:** a circle is a line that is made up of many points that are an equal distance from the centre point.

2. Draw 3 circles, each with a different diameter.
   a) Draw a circle by tracing around a circular object.
   b) Draw a circle using a pencil, pin and string.
   c) Draw a circle using your compasses.
   d) Measure the diameter of each circle using your ruler.

The Properties of a Circle

3. Fill in the names for the different parts of the circle.

   a) a = d_____

   b) b = r_____

   c) c = cir_____

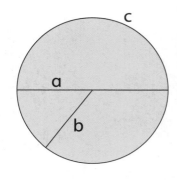

4. Complete the definitions for each of the parts of a circle.

   a) The line going from one side of a circle to another, passing through the _____ of the circle, is called the **diameter**.

   b) The line joining the _____ point to the _____ is called the **radius**.

   c) The _____ line around the circle is called the **circumference**.

5. Using your ruler, measure the diameter and radius of the circle above. Can you work out a relationship between them?

Strand: Shape and Space
Curriculum Objectives:
Identify the properties of the circle;
construct a circle of given radius or diameter;
plot simple co-ordinates and apply where appropriate;
use 2-D shapes and properties to solve problems.

Diameter = _____ radii (radii is the plural of radius).

6. What is the diameter of each of these circles?

    a) radius 4cm   b) radius 9cm   c) radius 3.5cm

    d) radius 7cm   e) radius 12.2cm   f) radius 6.8cm

7. Find the radius of each of these circles if the diameter is:

    a) 20cm   b) 15cm   c) 14.2cm

    d) 29cm   e) 18.4cm   f) 17cm

8. Using your compasses, construct circles with the following diameters on centimetre squared paper.

    a) 8cm   b) 9.4cm   c) 7.2cm   d) 3cm   e) 5cm

    f) Can you work out the approximate area of each circle by counting the squares?

9. What is the approximate area of this circle in cm²?

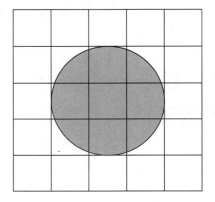

10. Using your compasses, construct circles with the following radii.

    a) 2cm   b) 3.5cm   c) 1.9cm   d) 4.1cm   e) 2.6cm

Circle Challenge

11. a) How many radii are in a diameter?

    b) Name the line that joins the centre point to the circumference of the circle.

    c) What is the name for the perimeter of a circle?

12. Using a piece of string, measure the circumference and diameter of each of these circles. Record your results in a table, as shown below.

A

B

D

C

Circle	Circumference	Diameter
A		
B		
C		
D		

13. Look at your results in the table in question 12 and decide approximately how many times bigger the circumference is than the diameter in each case.

14. Using a calculator, divide your circumference by your diameter for each of the circles in question 12. What do you notice?

15. Can you find an approximate circumference for circles with the following diameters?

   a) diameter = 6cm   b) diameter = 10cm   c) diameter = 9.1cm

16. Using a piece of string, measure the circumference of these objects. Note the diameter of each object too.

   a) jar   b) paint bottle

   c) cup   d) trundle wheel

17. Examine how these circle designs were made and try a few of your own.

   a)    b)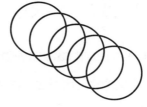

Symmetry

1. a) Which of these pictures are symmetrical?

   b) How many lines of symmetry can you find on each?

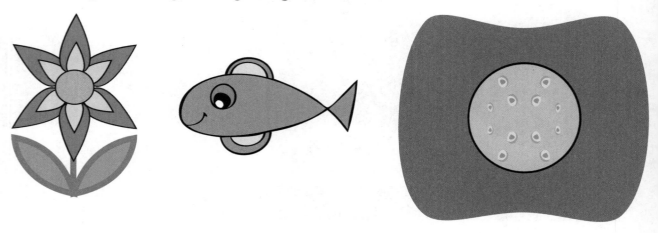

 Remember: a shape has line symmetry if it can be folded along a line so that each half fits exactly onto the other. Shapes which have lines or axes of symmetry are called symmetrical shapes.

2. Draw and cut out each of the following 2-D shapes:

   square   equilateral triangle   rectangle   trapezium   rhombus   pentagon

   a) How many different ways can you fold each shape evenly in half?

   b) Draw the shape into your copy and draw dotted lines where it has been folded.

   c) Record your results on a table like this.

Shape	Number of sides	Number of angles	Symmetrical? Yes or No	Number of lines of symmetry
square				

3. Which of these numbers are symmetrical?

   1   5   3   8   7   2   0

4. a) The number 1001 is symmetrical. How many lines of symmetry does it have?

   b) Can you think of other numbers that are symmetrical?

5. a) The word OXO is also symmetrical. How many lines of symmetry does it have?

    b) Can you think of any other words that might be symmetrical?

6. Draw the reflection of each of these shapes to make them symmetrical.

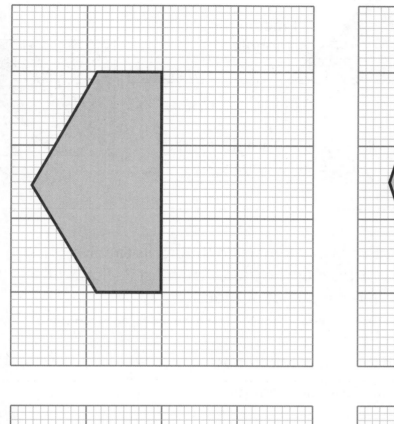

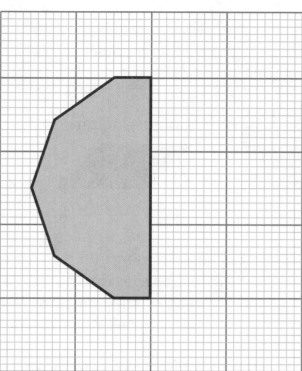

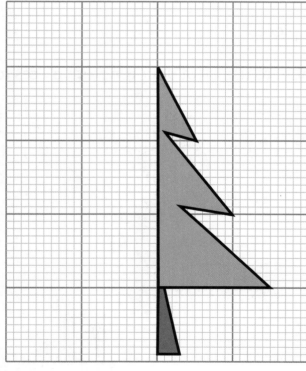

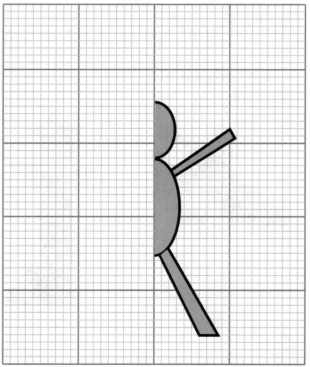

Tangrams

The tangram is a square that is cut up into 7 regular-shaped pieces. It was invented a long time ago in China. Each piece of the tangram is called a tan. The 7 tans are:

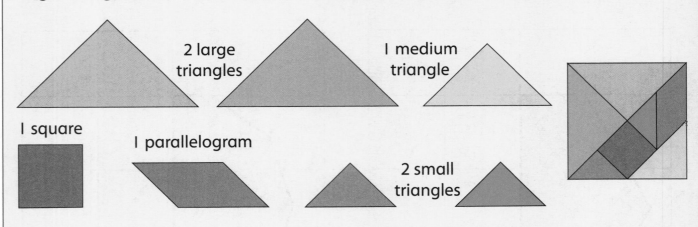

2 large triangles

1 medium triangle

1 square

1 parallelogram

2 small triangles

Remember: the classic rules when using tangrams to solve puzzles are that all 7 tans must be used, they must lie flat and they must touch but may not overlap.

1. Use the 7 tangram pieces to make the following shapes.

   a) square
   b) right-angled isosceles triangle
   c) hexagon

2. Can you form your age using your tangram pieces?

3. Have a go at making these pictures. Remember to use all of your tangram pieces for each picture.

Co-ordinates

The grid below is made up of rows and columns. The columns are represented by a letter and the rows are represented by a number. To work out what each square is called, first check to see what column it is in and then the row. For example, the red square is in column A and row 5, so that square is called A5.

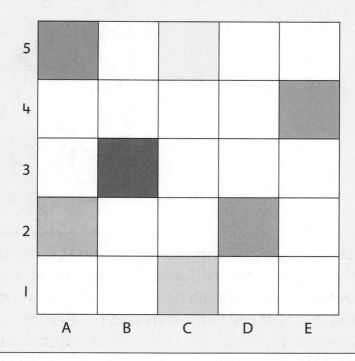

1. What would each of the coloured squares be called? (Remember to check the column first and then the row.)

   a) green   b) pink   c) yellow

   d) purple   e) blue   f) orange

2. Draw a grid like the one above in your copy, with 5 rows of 5 squares. Now colour in the following squares as directed.
   - Colour B5 and D5 blue.
   - Colour C3 red.
   - Colour A2, B1, C1, D1 and E2 green.

   a) What have you created?

   b) Design grid pictures of your own. Give the colouring directions to the people near you to see if they can recreate your masterpieces.

Battleship is a famous game that is played on a grid. Each player draws a grid and places their ships on it without the other person seeing. A battleship takes up 4 squares, a frigate 3 squares and a submarine 2 squares. You then take it in turns to call out squares (A5, G8, etc.) to see if you can find where the other person has hidden their ships. The first person to find all of the other person's squares wins.

3. In what section of the map would you find the following?

   a) pineapple   b) passion fruit
   c) kiwi   d) orange
   e) banana   f) watermelon

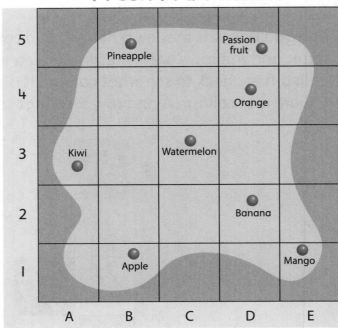

Fresh Fruit Island

Here is another type of grid. This time, instead of naming squares on the grid, we name points. We call these points **co-ordinates**. To work out what each point, or co-ordinate, is called, we refer to the numbers along the bottom and at the side. The line along the bottom of the grid is called the **x-axis** and the line up the side is called the **y-axis**. To name a point or co-ordinate, first check what number it is on the x-axis and then the y-axis. For example, the blue point on the grid is 3 on the x-axis and 5 on the y-axis, so we call that point (3, 5).

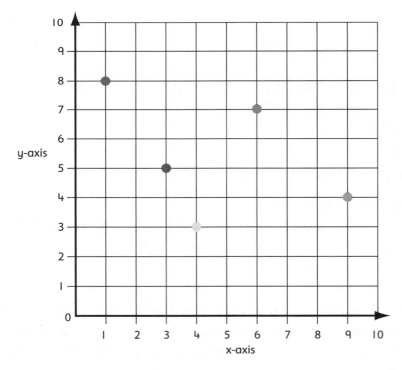

4. Can you name the co-ordinates of the other coloured points marked on the grid?

   a) red = (,)   b) green = (,)   c) yellow = (,)   d) orange = (,)

5. Mark these co-ordinates on a grid: (1, 2), (5, 4), (6, 1).
    Now use your ruler to draw lines to join the co-ordinates and make a triangle.
    Design triangles of your own by plotting co-ordinates and drawing them on a grid.

6. How many co-ordinates would you need to plot to create a quadrilateral?

7. Plot the following co-ordinates on a grid. What shapes have you created when you
    join the dots?
    a) (2, 1), (2, 4), (5, 4), (5, 1)   b) (7, 3), (10, 3), (10, 7), (7, 7)
    c) (2, 10), (6, 10), (1, 7), (5, 7)

Homework

1. Match these labels to the letters on the circle.

    radius   circumference   diameter

    A = _____

    B = _____

    C = _____

2. Using your compasses, construct circles with the following radii.
    a) 4cm   b) 6cm   c) 2.5cm   d) 1.5cm   e) 3.5cm

3. Using your compasses, construct circles with the following diameters.
    a) 7cm   b) 10cm   c) 9cm   d) 11cm   e) 8cm

4. Now use a piece of string to measure the circumferences of the circles you
    constructed in questions 2 and 3. In each case, divide the circumference by the
    diameter of that circle. Compare your answers.

5. a) Write the letters of your name in capital letters. How many of the letters in your
        name are symmetrical?

    b) Now try it for each of the names of the people in your family. Who has the most
        symmetrical letters in their name?

6. Using this font type, why is your MUM symmetrical but your DAD isn't?

7. Plot the following co-ordinates on a grid using an x-axis and a y-axis, then draw the shapes by joining the dots.

   a) (1, 4), (2, 2), (4, 3)
   b) (5, 2), (5, 5), (9, 2), (9, 5)
   c) (3, 6), (6, 6), (3, 9), (6, 9)

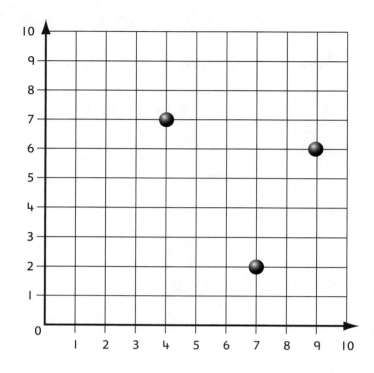

8. What are the co-ordinates of the points of the triangle marked on the grid?

Recap

- I know the properties of the circle.

- I know what symmetry is.

- I can identify and plot co-ordinates.

Talk About

Puzzler

What is the only factor that is common to both 18 and 25?

Find the HCF of 8 and 12.

What is the third multiple of 3?

What is the eighth multiple of 2?

What is the LCM of 5 and 25?

What is the LCM of 9 and 12?

Now write down each of the answers in sequence. What is the pattern?

Square Numbers

The number 4 can be arranged into exactly the same number of rows as columns.

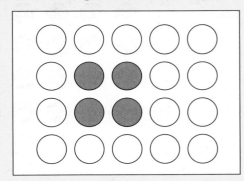

$$2 \times 2 = 4$$

1. Which of the following numbers can be arranged into the same number of rows and columns?

     9   18   25   36   42   16

Numbers that can be arranged into exactly the same number of rows and columns are called square numbers. What is the first square number?

We know that a square centimetre can be written as cm^2. So 4, which is 2×2, can be written as 2^2.

2. Fill in the blanks.

   a) $49 = \underline{\quad}^2$ b) $25 = \underline{\quad}^2$ c) $100 = \underline{\quad}^2$

   d) $64 = \underline{\quad}^2$ e) $36 = \underline{\quad}^2$ f) $121 = \underline{\quad}^2$

3. Now work out the answers to these. Use your calculator if necessary.

   a) 3^2 b) 9^2 c) 4^2 d) 12^2 e) 14^2 f) 18^2

   g) 23^2 h) 27^2 i) 34^2 j) 17^2 k) 29^2 l) 40^2

4. Is 15^2 exactly half of 30^2?

5. What is the 22nd square number?

Square Roots

This is a picture of the square number 49. How many rows and columns are there?

$$49 = 7 \times 7 = 7^2$$

The number of rows/columns (or the identical factors) is called the **square root** of a number. So the square root of 49 is 7.

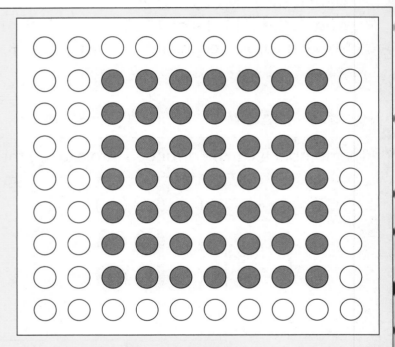

6. What is the square root of each of the following numbers?

   a) 36 b) 81 c) 144 d) 64 e) 25 f) 9

7. a) 4 is the square root of ___.   b) 10 is the square root of ___.

   c) 2 is the square root of ___.   d) 11 is the square root of ___.

> The symbol for the square root of a number is √.

Numbers Written in Exponential Form

We know that $2^2 = 2 \times 2 = 4$. But what would happen if we changed the raised number (the exponent) from 2 to 3?

$$2^3 = 2 \times 2 \times 2 = 8$$

So $2^3 = 8$.

What would 2^4 be?

$$2 \times 2 \times 2 \times 2 = 16$$

1. Now work out the value of these.

   a) 3^3 b) 4^3 c) 2^5 d) 12^2 e) 5^3 f) 3^4

   g) 6^3 h) 2^6 i) 4^4 j) 10^3 k) 7^3 l) 5^4

2. Use your calculator to work out the value of these.

   a) 9^3 b) 16^2 c) 3^5 d) 15^3 e) 4^5 f) 11^3

We know that $100 = 10 \times 10 = 10^2$.
If $1000 = 10 \times 10 \times 10 = 10^3$,
then $10000 = 10^4$
and $100000 = 10^5$.

3. A man bought 2^3 pencils, which cost 45c each. How much did the pencils cost him altogether?

4. The attendance at a football game was 5^5. How many people attended the game?

5. A charity sold 10^4 tickets for a concert to help raise money for homeless people. If the tickets cost €16, how much money did they raise?

Homework

1. Work out the value of these.

    a) 5^2 = _____
    b) 7^2 = _____
    c) 6^2 = _____
    d) 10^2 = _____
    e) 12^2 = _____
    f) 15^2 = _____
    g) 18^2 = _____
    h) 22^2 = _____
    i) 26^2 = _____
    j) 31^2 = _____
    k) 35^2 = _____
    l) 42^2 = _____

2. Fill in the blanks.

    a) 9 is the square root of _____.
    b) 3 is the square root of _____.
    c) 13 is the square root of _____.
    d) 16 is the square root of _____.
    e) 20 is the square root of _____.
    f) 24 is the square root of _____.

3. Now work out the value of these.

    a) 8^3
    b) 9^3
    c) 3^5
    d) 27^2
    e) 1^3
    f) 10^4

Recap

- I can identify square numbers. ◯ ◯ ◯

- I know what a square root is. ◯ ◯ ◯

- I know what numbers written in exponential form mean. ◯ ◯ ◯

 # Talk About

> **Remember:** a number sentence with an equals sign (=)
> is called an **equation**.
>
> We must equate, or equalise, the numbers on each side
> of the equals sign.

1. Try solving these equations.

   a) $179 + 283 =$ _____

   b) $654 - 92 =$ _____

   c) $8 \times 14 =$ _____

   d) $108 \div 12 =$ _____

   e) $6 = 126 \div$ _____

   f) $450 +$ _____ $= 982$

The blank in question 1 is a **variable** because it does not always represent the
same number. Instead of the blank, we can use another variable represented by a
letter.

For example, Sarah shared out her sweets among 6 of her friends. Each person got
12 sweets.

How many sweets did Sarah have at first?

Let x be the number of sweets Sarah had at first.

$$x \div 6 = 12$$
$$x = 72$$

Word Problems as Equations

1. Write an equation for each of these word problems. Don't forget to solve the equations.

    a) Paul had a large piece of wood and cut it into equal lengths of 45cm to make 5 shelves. How long was each shelf?

    b) Jennifer is 14 years old. She is 7 years younger than her brother Carl. What age is Carl?

    c) Jack had €25. After spending some money on a new shirt, he had €6.50 left. How much was the shirt?

    d) A train travelled 240km in 3 hours. What was the train's average speed per hour?

    e) Stephen bought 8 pens, which cost him a total of €4.40. How much was each pen?

    f) The length of a field is 105m and its width is 52m. Can you find the area of the field?

2. Devise some word problems for these equations.

    a) $x + 16 = 32$ b) $115 - y = 90$ c) $5 \times 11 = z$ d) $x \div 8 = 5$

3. Solve these equations.

    a) $y + 32 = 80$ b) $39 \div x = 13$ c) $200 - a = 116$

How would you solve this problem?

If Gillian was 4 times her age, she would be the same age as her mother, who is 48. What age is Gillian?

Let a = Gillian's age.
So $4 \times a = 48$, or $4a = 48$.
If $4a = 48$, then $a = 12$.
So Gillian is 12 years old.

---

4. Solve these problems by writing equations and finding the value of the variable.

    a) Trevor has €14. If he had €2 more, he would have twice the amount of money that Joe has. How much money does Joe have? (Let the amount of money John has = y, so $14 + 2 = 2y$.)

    b) A building is 4 times taller than Vanessa. If the building is 5.8 metres high, how tall is Vanessa?

    c) Orla wants to upgrade her laptop. Her current computer runs at 1.5GHz and the latest model runs 2.5 times faster. How fast does the new computer run?

    d) Ann gets half her age in euro as pocket money. If she gets €6 pocket money, what age is Ann?

5. The length of a runway is 150 times its width. If the width of the runway is 6 metres, how long is the runway?

6. Write word problems for these equations.

    a) $4x = 32$ (for example: If 4 apples cost 32c, how much does 1 apple cost?)

    b) $y + 5 = 25$ c) $5z - 7 = 33$ d) $€81 ÷ 9 = x$

7. Robert is going on holiday to England. The current exchange rate is 1.5 euro to 1 pound sterling. Formulate an equation to help you complete this table.

Euro (€)	Sterling (£)
10	
50	
75	
110	
	195
215	

Puzzler

Derek walks to school every day. If he walks a total of 35km each week, how long is his journey to school?

Make sure you consider all aspects of this problem carefully before working out your answer.

If he walked a total of 732km during the course of the whole school year, what information would you need to have to help you work out the answer? When you have that information, work out the answer.

8. Write an equation for each of the tables and use it to help you fill in the gaps.
   For example: Table A: Let the numbers in Column A be represented by y.
   We multiply each number by 2 to get the numbers in Column B.
   So the equation will read   y × 2 = Column B
                                                  or for the first number, 1 × 2 = 2.

a) **Table A**

1	2
2	4
3	
4	
5	10
10	
12	
15	
20	
100	

b) **Table B**

1	5
2	10
3	
4	
10	
13	65
18	
20	
35	
50	

c) **Table C**

1	16
2	
3	
4	19
5	
20	
25	
40	
60	
100	

d) **Table D**

1	76
2	
3	
4	
5	80
15	
35	
50	
75	
150	

Solving One-step Equations

1. Solve these equations.

   a) $56 + a = 132$ b) $x \div 5 = 17$ c) $328 - b = 120$

2. For each of the following buses, write an equation to calculate how many people were on the bus before the first stop.

   a) **Green bus**
   At the first stop, 7 people got on and then there  were 42. How many people were there at first?

   b) **Blue bus**
   At the first stop, 12 people got off and then there were 61.  How many were there at first?

   c) **Yellow bus**
   At the first stop, the number doubled and  then there were 86. How many people were there at first?

   d) **Red bus**
   At the first stop, the number halved and then  there were 34. How many people were there at first?

3. Pick the right equation for the problem.

a) 7 added to x is equal to 12. $7x = 12$ $7 - x = 12$ $7 + x = 12$

b) y multiplied by 6 is equal to 30. $y + 6 = 30$ $6 \times y = 30$ $6 \div y = 30$

c) z taken from 18 is equal to 5. $z - 18 = 5$ $18 - z = 5$ $18 - 5 = z$

d) 56 divided by y is equal to 7. $56 \div y = 7$ $y \div 56 = 7$ $7 \div y = 56$

e) Now work out the answers for each.

4. Write an equation to help you solve each of these.

a) Eoin thought of a number and added 39 to it. He then had 421. What number did Eoin think of?

b) Maura thought of a number, divided it by 9 and then had 91. What number did she think of?

c) Devise 3 of your own riddles to puzzle your classmates.

5. The table shows the goals scored for some of the teams in a school soccer league.

Teams	Terriers	Alsatians	Wolves	Hounds	Labradors
Goals scored	8				16

Change each of the questions to equations to work out the rest of the teams' scores.

a) The Alsatians scored 6 goals more than the Terriers.

b) The Wolves scored half as many goals as the Alsatians, or 1 goal less than the Terriers.

c) If you multiply the Wolves' score by 3 and take away 4, you will get how many goals the Hounds scored.

d) Skilful Sam scored a lot of goals for the Terriers. You can work out how many he scored by dividing the Terriers' score by 2. How many goals did he score?

e) Which team scored the most goals?

6. Solve the following equations using your calculator.
   a) $5679 + x = 11236$
   b) $y - 9830 = 4097$
   c) $62.85\text{kg} \times a = 942.75\text{kg}$
   d) $9856\text{km} \div z = 704\text{km}$
   e) $€232.50 + y = €798.60$
   f) $b \times 2.56 \text{ litres} = 218.88 \text{ litres}$

7. Complete these multiplication tables.

a)

×	9	12	7	15	8
5					
11					
6					
3					
4					

b)

×					
	16	40	80	88	72
	6	15	30	33	27
	14	35	70	77	63
	12	30	60	66	54
	2	5	10	11	9

Homework

1. Solve these equations.
   a) $14 + x = 73$
   b) $22 \times a = 176$
   c) $b - 148 = 127$
   d) $c \div 7 = 29$
   e) $198 - y = 49$
   f) $b + 129 = 401$

2. Write equations for these word problems and then solve them.
   a) Betty bought a bit of butter (75g, to be precise). If the price of butter was 3c per gram, how much was the bit of butter that Betty bought?
   b) Tommy tidied his 136 toy cars into 4 storage boxes. If he put the same number of cars in each box, how many were in each box?
   c) If 13426 people live in a town and 7689 are female, how many are male?
   d) Miserly Mick had €19024 and he decided out of the goodness of his heart to give his nephew €19 and his niece €17. How much money did he have left for himself?
   e) Make up 2 of your own to try out on your classmates.

3. Work out what the variable is in each of these.
   a) $5a = 4720$
   b) $8b = 2152$
   c) $11c = 5445$
   d) $16d = 2784$
   e) $27e = 4941$
   f) $48f = 4608$

4. Use your calculator to work out these equations.

   a) $a - 4927 = 11678$

   b) $b + 13176 = 27005$

   c) $49c = 6125$

   d) $d \div 124 = 744$

Recap

- I can write and solve word problems as equations. ○ ○ ○
- I can write and solve equations. ○ ○ ○

Talk About

> The decimal system of writing numbers is the system we use to record whole numbers and fractions. It's called the decimal system because it's organised to the base number 10.

1. Complete this true or false quiz and then compare your answers with your friends.

    999.999

    a) In the decimal system, whole numbers and fractions are separated by the decimal point.

    b) The decimal point never moves.

    c) In the above number, each 9 is 10 times bigger than the one immediately to its right.

    d) In the above number, each 9 is 10 times smaller than the one immediately to its left.

    e) All fractions can be written as decimals.

    f) If you divide the numerator by the denominator of any fraction, you will find out what that fraction is as a decimal.

Comparing Fractions and Decimals

2. Change these fractions to decimal fractions.

    a) $\frac{6}{10}$ b) $\frac{3}{100}$ c) $\frac{29}{100}$ d) $\frac{8}{1000}$

    e) $\frac{87}{1000}$ f) $\frac{941}{1000}$ g) $\frac{43}{10}$ h) $\frac{189}{100}$

> **Remember:** sometimes we have to find an equivalent fraction with 10, 100 or 1000 as the denominator so that we can write the fraction as a decimal.

Strand: Number
Curriculum Objectives:
Compare and order fractions and decimals;
estimate sums, differences, products and quotients of decimals;
add and subtract decimals (to three decimal places) without

multiply and divide a decimal number by a
decimal, without and with a calculator;
solve problems involving operations with fractio

112

3. Find equivalent fractions for these and then write them as decimals.
   a) $\frac{1}{2}$
   b) $\frac{2}{5}$
   c) $\frac{1}{4}$
   d) $\frac{4}{5}$
   e) $\frac{3}{4}$
   f) $\frac{3}{5}$
   g) $\frac{7}{20}$
   h) $\frac{1}{8}$

4. Now write these decimals as fractions in their lowest terms.
   a) 0.8
   b) 0.25
   c) 0.15
   d) 0.46
   e) 0.85
   f) 0.96
   g) 0.375
   h) 0.625

5. Put the following decimals in order, starting with the lowest value.
   a) 8.14, 8.41, 1.48, 4.81
   b) 21.59, 25.19, 21.95, 25.91
   c) 6.242, 6.224, 6.422, 6.222
   d) 1.756, 1.576, 1.6, 1.657
   e) 209.4, 204.9, 240.9, 249

Remember: when we add or subtract decimals, we keep the decimal points directly underneath each other. This ensures that the units, $\frac{1}{10}$s, etc. are always directly underneath each other. We can use 0s as placeholders.

Adding and Subtracting Decimals

Jim drank 2.345 litres of water on Monday, 1.83 litres of water on Tuesday and 3.4 litres on Wednesday. How much water did he drink over the 3 days?

We write the numbers underneath each other, keeping the decimal points directly underneath each other and using 0s as placeholders.

$$\begin{array}{r} 2.345 \\ 1.830 \\ + 3.400 \\ \hline 7.575 \end{array}$$

Jim drank 7.575 litres of water over the 3 days.

1. Now work out these decimal additions. Remember to put the decimal points directly underneath each other and use 0s as placeholders.
   a) 2.467 + 36.8 + 0.79
   b) 132.2 + 71.18 + 0.957
   c) 5.35 + 198.356 + 28.7
   d) 7.089 + 56.6 + 2.365
   e) 0.978 + 64.06 + 1.638
   f) 57.9 + 9.259 + 5.89

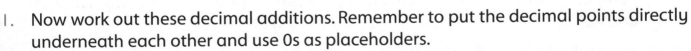

We do the same when we're subtracting as we do when we're adding. We keep the decimal points directly underneath each other and use 0s as placeholders.

Tim weighs 52.46kg and his twin brother, Tom, weighs 49.894kg. How much lighter is Tom than Tim?

Again, we write the numbers underneath each other, keeping the decimal points directly underneath each other and using 0s as placeholders.

$$
\begin{array}{r}
{}^{4}\,{}^{1}1\,{}^{1}3\,{}^{1}5\,{}^{1} \\
5\,2\,.\,4\,6\,0 \\
-\ 4\,9\,.\,8\,9\,4 \\
\hline
0\,2\,.\,5\,6\,6
\end{array}
$$

So Tom is 2.566kg lighter than Tim.

2. Can you subtract these?

a) 28.5 – 6.98
b) 47.34 – 28.8
c) 1.68 – 0.795
d) 83.1 – 19.462
e) 12.312 – 9.59
f) 638.425 – 287.6

> If the numbers are written in different formats, change them all to decimals and add or subtract, as appropriate.

3. Richard was competing in the triple jump. In the hop phase he travelled 5.83m, in the skip phase he travelled $4\frac{3}{4}$m and in the jump phase he travelled 6m 27cm. How long was his overall jump?

4. Jenny was competing in the high jump. Her best jump was 17cm short of her lifetime best jump, which was 1.83m. How high did she jump in the competition?

Multiplying Decimals

5. Do these multiplication questions using your calculator.

a) 6.5 × 10
b) 2.152 × 100
c) 17.69 × 10
d) 4.623 × 1000
e) 30.65 × 10
f) 0.519 × 100

g) Compare the answer you got in each case with your original number. What do you notice?

h) Remembering that the decimal point never moves, what rule can we make for multiplying decimals by 10, 100 or 1000?

6. Now use your rule to find the answers to these without using your calculator.

a) 0.68 × 10
b) 2.254 × 100
c) 7.095 × 1000
d) 4.379 × 1000
e) 34.96 × 10
f) 6.04 × 100

Barry has €4.27 in his piggy bank. His sister, Anne, has 6 times more money than Barry. How much money does Anne have?

When multiplying a decimal number by a whole number, we must remember to make sure to put the decimal point in the answer directly below the decimal point in the number.

$$
\begin{array}{r}
4.27 \\
\times \quad {}_1{}_4 6 \\
\hline
25.62
\end{array}
$$

So Anne has €25.62 in her piggy bank.

7. Now try these, remembering to put in the decimal point.
   a) 1.59×7
   b) 98.4×5
   c) 5.186×6
   d) 47.04×8
   e) 975.7×4
   f) 2.861×9
   g) 8.23×12
   h) 0.869×3
   i) 34.65×11

Mr Power's 5th class is going to Dublin on a day trip. The DART ticket costs €1.34 return per child. There are 32 children in the class. What will the total bill for the children be?

(2 decimal places)

$$
\begin{array}{r}
1.34 \\
\times \quad 32 \\
\hline
268 \\
40{\overset{\shortmid}{2}}0 \\
\hline
42.88
\end{array}
$$

(2 decimal places)

8. Try these. Check your answers with a calculator.
   a) 26.4×27
   b) 0.73×38
   c) 15.95×19
   d) 3.617×42
   e) 1.935×24
   f) 85.9×68

9. Every step that Lisa takes is 0.73m. If she takes 59 steps, how far has she travelled?

10. Shane uses 7.048 litres of water every morning for his shower. How much water did he use altogether over a 2-week period?

11. If one packet of Stat Attack cards costs €1.45, how much would 78 packets cost?

12. The journey from Sarah's house to her school is 7km 83m. If she was absent on Tuesday, how far did she travel to and from school over the course of the week?

Dividing Decimals

1. Remember what happened and the rule you made when you multiplied decimals by 10, 100 or 1000. What do you think will happen when you divide decimals by 10, 100 or 1000?

   Make up a rule and try it out on these division questions.
   a) $23.4 \div 10$
   b) $309.7 \div 100$
   c) $386.9 \div 10$
   d) $476.1 \div 1000$
   e) $3.83 \div 10$
   f) $57.2 \div 100$
   g) $719.26 \div 100$
   h) $294.3 \div 1000$
   i) $1.2 \div 100$
   j) Check your answers with a calculator to see if your rule worked.

The dressmaker cut a length of ribbon that was 1.84m into 4 pieces of equal length. How long was each piece of ribbon?

Again, as when we multiplied a decimal number by a whole number, we must remember to put the decimal point in the answer directly underneath where it is in the original number.

$$4 \, \overline{| \, 1.8\overset{2}{4}}$$
$$ \, 0.46$$

So each piece of ribbon is 0.46m or 46cm long.

---

2. Now try these.
   a) $0.96 \div 6$
   b) $35.6 \div 4$
   c) $4.735 \div 5$
   d) $28.62 \div 9$
   e) $0.896 \div 7$
   f) $214.4 \div 8$
   g) $21.45 \div 11$
   h) $1.704 \div 3$
   i) $555.6 \div 12$

There are 24 sweets in a box with a total weight of 0.936kg. If each sweet is exactly the same weight, how heavy is each sweet?

$$
\begin{array}{r}
0.039 \\
24 \, \overline{| \, 0.936} \\
- \, 0.720 \\
\hline
216 \\
- \, 216 \\
\hline
000
\end{array}
$$

So each sweet weighs 0.039kg

---

3. Try these. Check your answers with a calculator.
   a) $587.2 \div 16$
   b) $4.176 \div 24$
   c) $90.24 \div 32$
   d) $636.4 \div 43$
   e) $97.25 \div 25$
   f) $13.243 \div 19$

4. Share €181.16 evenly among 28 people.

5. Shirley has 2.775 litres of pink lemonade for her birthday party to share evenly amongst her 15 guests. How much lemonade will each of her guests get?

6. 48 CDs weighed 8.88kg in total. How much did each individual CD weigh?

7. 29 people carried the Olympic torch from Dublin to Belfast. If the distance between Dublin and Belfast is 104.4km and each person carried the torch the same distance, how far did each person run with the torch?

Multiplying Decimals by Decimals

John's flask holds 1.29 litres of soup. James's flask holds 1.6 times more soup than John's. How much soup does James' flask hold?

We multiply in exactly the same way as we did before. The only difference will be where the decimal point goes in the answer.

$$
\begin{array}{r}
1.29 \\
\times \quad 1.6 \\
{\scriptstyle 1\ 5} \\
\hline
774 \\
+ \ 1290 \\
\hline
2.064 \\
\end{array}
$$

2 places of decimals
1 place of decimals

3 places of decimals

How would you make a rule for this?

1. Now try these. Make sure to put your decimal point in the right place in your answer. Check your answers with a calculator.

a) 2.38 × 1.4

b) 76.4 × 0.18

c) 69.7 × 2.3

d) 0.58 × 4.8

e) 81.7 × 0.35

f) 3.18 × 4.9

g) 178.2 × 0.26

h) 0.79 × 7.6

i) 25.38 × 3.7

Dividing Decimals by Decimals

What about when we have to divide a decimal number by another decimal number?

Sonia ran 1.7 laps of the park and a total of 6.205km. How long was each lap of the park?

To work this out, we have to divide 1.7 into 6.205. To make it easier for ourselves, we can multiply both numbers by 10.

$$1.7 \times 10 = 17 \qquad\qquad 6.205 \times 10 = 62.05$$

Because we've done the same thing to both numbers, our final answer will still be the same except now we're dividing by 17 and not by a number with a decimal in it. So we can do as we did before.

```
            03.65
    17 | 62.05
       − 51.00
         ‾‾‾‾‾‾
         11.05
       − 10.20
         ‾‾‾‾‾‾
         00.85
       − 00.85
         ‾‾‾‾‾‾
         00.00
```

So each lap of the park was 3.65km long.

1. Now try these – remember to multiply both numbers by either 10 or 100 to make sure you are dividing by a whole number. Check your answers with a calculator.

a) $4.524 \div 2.6$
b) $6.516 \div 0.18$
c) $0.5775 \div 0.35$

d) $64.53 \div 2.7$
e) $15.732 \div 0.36$
f) $5.394 \div 2.9$

Puzzler

Jane was practising for the Dublin marathon. The week before the marathon she ran 0.875 of the 40km course in a time of 2 hours 55 minutes. Running at the same speed, how long would it take her to complete the full course?

A string of sausages is 1.82m long. If each sausage is 0.13m long, how many sausages make up the string?

Remember: first we multiply by 100 to make sure we are dividing by a whole number.

0.13 × 100 = 13   1.82 × 100 = 182

```
        014
   13 | 182
        130 –
      _____
        052
        052 –
      _____
        000
```

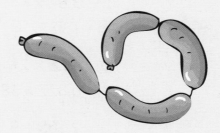

What do you notice about the answer? The answer 14 is bigger than the number we started with, even though we are dividing. Why do you think that is?

2. Darren wanted to buy dry-wipe markers for his whiteboard. If each marker cost €0.95, how many markers could he buy for €26.60?

3. 1 bag of pasta weighs 0.675kg. How much would 18 bags of pasta weigh?

4. Frank's house has a floor area of 107.8 square metres. If Julie's house is 1.4 times bigger than Frank's, how big is Julie's house?

5. A delivery van brought 227.5kg of potatoes to a supermarket. If the potatoes were in bags each weighing 6.5kg, how many bags did the van deliver?

Homework

1. Change these fractions to decimal fractions.

    a) $\frac{5}{10}$ b) $\frac{19}{100}$ c) $\frac{63}{1000}$ d) $\frac{7}{100}$

    e) $\frac{198}{1000}$ f) $\frac{2}{5}$ g) $\frac{3}{4}$ h) $\frac{13}{20}$

2. Change these decimals to fractions and write them in their lowest terms.

    a) 0.16   b) 0.8   c) 0.25   d) 0.8

    e) 0.22   f) 0.55   g) 0.44   h) 0.125

3. Put the following decimals in order, starting with the highest in value.

    a) 3.26, 2.36, 3.62, 2.63   b) 1.583, 1.385, 1.853, 1.538

    c) 87.14, 87.41, 84.17, 84.71   d) 6.367, 6.763, 6.376, 6.637

4. a) $64.8 + 0.954 + 7.36$
   b) $17.309 + 64.92 + 257.1$
   c) $2.185 + 0.86 + 78.4$
   d) $9.426 + 0.57 + 382.5$
   e) $47.208 + 4.65 + 19.07$
   f) $38.7 + 0.597 + 481.26$

5. a) $4.3 - 2.65$
   b) $27.38 - 16.736$
   c) $307.2 - 95.87$
   d) $1.19 - 0.589$
   e) $7.352 - 4.53$
   f) $416.08 - 87.435$

6. a) 0.98×8
   b) 3.67×6
   c) 47.4×11
   d) 56.19×9
   e) 18.372×7
   f) 0.377×12

7. a) 2.97×16
   b) 43.8×27
   c) 1.509×34
   d) 73.6×29
   e) 0.827×38
   f) 58.3×45

8. a) $15.54 \div 6$
   b) $2.565 \div 9$
   c) $198.4 \div 4$
   d) $29.52 \div 8$
   e) $384.5 \div 5$
   f) $0.588 \div 7$

9. a) $18.75 \div 15$
   b) $8.328 \div 24$
   c) $539.6 \div 19$
   d) $12.936 \div 28$
   e) $188.48 \div 31$
   f) $1949.9 \div 37$

10. a) 7.36×1.4
    b) 25.83×1.8
    c) 84.9×0.23
    d) 16.24×7.9
    e) 37.6×0.47
    f) 148.1×0.53

11. a) $3.672 \div 1.7$
    b) $13.962 \div 0.26$
    c) $16.812 \div 0.18$
    d) $11.115 \div 3.9$
    e) $13.508 \div 4.4$
    f) $15.295 \div 0.35$

12. If a bus route is 37.409km in length and the driver travels it 18 times a day, how far does he travel each day?

13. If 1 lollipop costs €0.36 and Toothless Terry spent €21.24 in total, how many lollipops did he buy?

14. If last year's Christmas tree was 1.9m tall and this year's tree is 1.3 times taller, how tall is this year's Christmas tree?

Recap

- I can write fractions as decimals and vice versa. ○ ○ ○

- I can add and subtract decimals. ○ ○ ○

- I can multiply and divide decimals. ○ ○ ○

- I can multiply decimals by decimals. ○ ○ ○

- I can divide decimals by decimals. ○ ○ ○

 # Talk About

1. Can you write these cent amounts as decimals of a euro?
   a) 85c
   b) 174c
   c) 3c
   d) 925c
   e) 1560c
   f) 3999c
   g) 10482c
   h) 65530c
   i) 269849c

2. What is the least number of coins possible to make these amounts of money?
   a) €1.35
   b) €0.92
   c) €2.50
   d) €4.81
   e) €7.99
   f) €9.11

3. Calculate the change you would get out of €20 after spending the following.
   a) €1.50 + €12.80
   b) €4.95 + €6.25
   c) €2.20 + €3.99 + €8.10
   d) €3.55 + € 16.40
   e) €2.56 × 4
   f) €5.60 × 3
   g) €1.80 × 9
   h) (€6.40 × 2) + €5.15
   i) (€3.10 × 4) + €2.50

Getting Value for Money

4. Lisa is buying some CDs and has been given these options. Which option is better value? Work it out using the unitary method or by finding the price of 1 unit.

5. The Walsh family from Dublin have decided to travel to Cork to visit some relatives. They have collected information about a few different ways to travel and the cost of each and need to decide which is the best value.

   a) Help them decide by working out the total amount for each option.

Train	**Bus**	**Plane**
Fare: Return	Fare: Return	Fare: Return
Adult: €42	Adult: €28	Adult: € 90
Child: €21	Child: €18	Child: € 40

   b) If there are 2 adults and 3 children in the Walsh family, work out the cost for each option (train, bus and plane).

   c) Which is the best-value option for their trip?

Think About

2 friends are playing cards for 20c a game. At the end, Tim has won 2 games and Denis is €1.20 up. How many games did they play altogether?

Calculating Bills

1. It's Anne's first day working at Betty's Books and there are various special offers running in the shop at the moment. Help Anne to calculate some customers' shopping bills.

Betty's Books

Posters €4.00
Buy 1 poster - get second half price

Spend €100 or more - get 10% discount

OPEN

Buy all 5 best-selling novels - get 25% off

Do-it-yourself range of books €12.00

Top 5 best-selling novels €15.00 each

Educational computer software €10.00

Gel pens €1.50

DVDs €19.50

DIY for Beginners

New release audio books €18.00 each

Inter-active Maths

All prices exclude VAT

Remember: VAT does not apply to books, but all other items in the shop will have to have VAT @ 20% added to the price.

a) Karen's items: 1 best-selling novel, 2 do-it-yourself books. What is the total bill?

b) Daniel's items: 2 posters, 3 gel pens, 1 educational computer software. What is the total bill?

c) Jim's items: 2 DVDs. What is the total bill?

d) Valerie's items: Top 5 best-selling novels. What is the total bill?

e) Tom's items: 3 DVDs, 2 audio books, 1 educational computer software. What is the total bill?

f) Rachel's items: 1 best-selling novel, 1 poster and 2 educational computer software. What is the total bill?

g) Calculate Rachel's change out of €50.

h) Choose the items you would buy if you had €30. Remember to include VAT or discounts if they apply. What change would you get?

Money in Different Countries

1. a) What currency do we use in Ireland?
   b) How many countries have the euro as their currency?
   c) What are the benefits of using the euro?
   d) Name 3 other major currencies in use in the world today.

2. If you were in the following countries, what currency would you be using?
   a) Britain   b) France   c) United States   d) Japan

3. a) If you were travelling to a country that did not use the euro, where would you get the currency you need?
   b) Where could you find out how much of the new currency you would get for your euros?

The amount of any currency we would get when changing from one currency to another is called the **exchange rate** and can vary from day to day.

4. Find and copy today's exchange rates in a newspaper or online. Discuss the rates with the person beside you. How many US dollars is the euro worth today?

Here is an example of a euro exchange rate. Using the rates, work out the following questions.

For example: How many pounds sterling would you get for €10?

$$€1 = £0.86,$$
$$so €10 = 10 \times 0.86 = £8.60$$

US dollar	1.34
Japanese yen	103.02
Pound sterling	0.86
Swiss franc	1.23
Russian rouble	43.32
Australian dollar	1.37
Canadian dollar	1.39
Chinese yuan renminbi	8.54
New Zealand dollar	1.73
South African rand	10.70

5. Calculate how much of each of the other currencies you would get for:
    a) €10
    b) €100

6. a) If you were travelling to the USA and wanted to change €200, how many US dollars would you get?
    b) What would €50 give you in Japanese yen?
    c) If you were travelling to Switzerland and bought €250 worth of Swiss francs, how many francs would you have?
    d) How many Australian dollars would you get for €1000?
    e) Invent a few of your own currency exchanges.

7. Find the symbol for each of the different currencies listed in the table above.

8. Change these euro amounts to the following currencies. Use the exchange rates from the table above.
    a) €250 to pounds sterling
    b) €600 to Japanese yen
    c) €550 to US dollars
    d) €2000 to Canadian dollars
    e) €3400 to Australian dollars

Orla's pen pal, Chelsea, is coming to Ireland from Boston for 3 weeks. She wants to exchange $335 US dollars to euro. How many euro will she get for her money?

$$\$335 \text{ to euro} = 335 \div 1.34$$
$$\text{(dollar exchange rate)} = €250$$

Bureau de Change

9. Change the following currencies to euro. Check your answers on your calculator.

a) US $670

b) £774

c) CAN $417

d) AUS $548

e) US $1005

f) £1558

Complete these questions using your calculator. Round your answer to the nearest cent.

10. An Australian tourist in Ireland bought a digital camera for €630. How much would this be in Australian dollars?

11. A brand new sports car costs £21300 + VAT at 21% in London. How much is this in total in euro?

12. Exclusive yacht for sale: only AUS $22346.50. How much would it cost to buy this yacht in euro?

13. A villa in the south of France costs €750000. A Canadian businesswoman is looking at buying it. Help her convert the price to Canadian dollars.

14. Want to buy a fabulous ranch in Texas? A steal at just US$1187500! How much is the ranch in euro?

Homework

The Joyce family are embarking on an adventurous round-the-world trip. There are 2 adults and 3 children in the family. They plan to travel through Europe and Asia to Australia, where they will spend 3 weeks in Sydney, and then on to San Francisco for a week, New York for a week and finally home across the Atlantic Ocean.

1. Plot the Joyce family's trip around the world using your atlas or a world map.

2. For their stay in Australia, they exchange €1500. How many Australian dollars will they get for this?

3. While in Australia, the family go on an action-packed day trip out to sea, with diving, fishing and whale watching as part of the day. It costs $20 for an adult and $8 for a child.

a) What is the total cost in Australian dollars for the day?

b) How much is this total in euro?

4. The family have brought US$1000 in travellers' cheques, which they exchange for cash in San Francisco. How much did these travellers' cheques cost them in euro?

5. On an evening out, the Joyces ate in an exclusive restaurant. Have a look at the menu and answer the following questions.

Menu

FANCY FOOD

Succulent steak	$26
Luscious lobster	$34
Fabulous fajitas	$17
Perfect pizza	$15
Gorgeous goujons	$13

SUMPTIOUS SIDES

Fabulous fries	$4
Magnificent mash	$6
Rip-roaring roast potatoes	$5
Glorious greens	$3
Sensational salad	$8

DELICIOUS DESSERTS

Incredible ice cream	$7
Posh pavlova	$9
Seriously sticky toffee pudding	$11

BRILLIANT BEVERAGES

Cool cola	$4
Chic champagne	$43
OMG orange juice	$7
Wicked wine	$29

a) How much would a glass of orange juice cost in euro?

b) Sally ate steak with roast potatoes and had a bottle of cola to drink. What was the total cost of her meal in dollars? What was the total cost in euro?

c) Mr and Mrs Joyce both had lobster and 1 bottle of champagne. Find the total cost in both dollars and euro.

d) Choose a meal you would like from the menu and work out the total price, both in dollars and euro.

Recap

- I can calculate value for money.
- I can work out total bills.
- I can convert euro to foreign currencies.
- I can convert foreign currencies to euro.

Talk About

Peter was playing darts. With his first dart he scored 17, with his second 8 and with his third 15. What was his total score?

Obviously you will add the 3 scores to get the total, but does the order in which you add them matter?

$$17 + 8 + 15 = ?$$

If I add 17 and 8 first, I get 25. $\quad 25 + 15 = ?$
If I add 8 and 15 first, I get 23. $\quad 17 + 23 = ?$

Are both the answers the same?
What conclusion can we draw?

Susan collects spiders. She had 28 altogether, but yesterday 9 of them escaped and today a further 6 escaped. How many spiders does Susan have left?

$$28 - 9 - 6 = ?$$

Does it matter in which order I subtract?

If I subtract 9 from 28 first, I get 19. $\quad 19 - 6 = ?$
If I subtract 6 from 9 first, I get 3. $\quad 28 - 3 = ?$

Are both the answers the same? What conclusion can we draw?

Brackets help clear up the confusion. We always do the operation inside the brackets first.

$$\text{So } 93 - (47 + 25) = ? \qquad \text{becomes} \qquad 93 - 72 = ?$$

Using Brackets

1. Work out these in your head.

   a) $42 \div (36 \div 6)$

   b) $9 \times (4 \times 3)$

   c) $(27 - 19) \times 7$

   d) $(35 \div 7) \times 8$

   e) $4 \times (39 - 27)$

   f) $(12 \times 6) \div 9$

   g) $(38 + 46) \div 12$

   h) $(7 \times 9) - 47$

   i) $11 \times (4 \times 2)$

2. Now try these. (You don't have to do them in your head – unless, of course, you want to!)

   a) $(34 + 28) \times 3$

   b) $176 \times (63 - 45)$

   c) $342 - (79 + 153)$

   d) $147 \div (53 - 46)$

   e) $1274 + (347 \times 6)$

   f) $4009 - (5913 - 3685)$

   g) $(159 \times 43) - 3945$

   h) $3471 + (237 \times 26)$

   i) $5028 + (2974 + 1579)$

   j) $4682 + (4747 - 859)$

   k) $(27 \times 19) \times 35$

   l) $246 \times (225 \div 9)$

When There Are No Brackets

When there are no brackets to tell us which operation to perform first, how do we decide? Can you remember the order in which the operations are to be done? Here's a hint:

BODMAS

Discuss with the people near you what you think that word might mean.

Now write the order in which you should perform the operations if there are no brackets.

1st _____   2nd _____

3rd _____   4th _____

3. Now try these.

   a) $76 \times 24 + 2706$

   b) $193 - 678 \div 6$

   c) $8032 - 154 \times 36$

   d) $1637 + 3924 - 2576$

   e) $342 \times 552 \div 8$

   f) $882 \div 7 + 469$

4. Use your calculator for these.

   a) $12345 + 17054 - 18872$

   b) $2047 \div 23 \times 176$

   c) $11736 - 239 \times 38$

   d) $4715 + 524 \times 28$

Missing Operators

1. Put the correct symbols into these.

   a) $8 + (9 \underline{\quad} 6) = 23$ b) $(4 \times 2) \underline{\quad} 3 = 24$ c) $(9 - 5) \underline{\quad} 7 = 11$

   d) $12 \underline{\quad} (33 \div 11) = 4$ e) $(7 \underline{\quad} 5) - 10 = 25$ f) $36 \div (8 \underline{\quad} 4) = 3$

   g) $24 - (17 \underline{\quad} 9) = 16$ h) $(42 \div 6) \underline{\quad} 9 = 63$ i) $8 \times (10 \underline{\quad} 2) = 64$

But what if both operators are missing, like in this one?

$$14 \underline{\quad} (5 \underline{\quad} 2) = 2$$

There are lots more possibilities now. We can narrow down the possibilities by using common sense.
   - Both symbols will not be × because the answer is too small.
   - Both symbols will not be + because the answer is too small.
   - If we look at the first number and the answer, we get a very good idea.

What must you do to 14 to get an answer of 2?

$$14 \div 7 = 2$$

We know that the operation inside the brackets must give us an answer of 7.
You should now know what symbol to use.

2. Try these.

   a) $7 \underline{\quad} (4 \underline{\quad} 5) = 63$ b) $9 \underline{\quad} (3 \underline{\quad} 6) = 18$ c) $32 \underline{\quad} (4 \underline{\quad} 2) = 4$

   d) $6 \underline{\quad} (2 \underline{\quad} 5) = 60$ e) $7 \underline{\quad} (9 \underline{\quad} 3) = 21$ f) $21 \underline{\quad} (15 \underline{\quad} 6) = 12$

   g) $45 \underline{\quad} (5 \underline{\quad} 4) = 5$ h) $6 \underline{\quad} (14 \underline{\quad} 5) = 54$ i) $11 \underline{\quad} (84 \underline{\quad} 7) = 132$

3. Now use your calculator to work out the missing symbols.

   a) $19 \underline{\quad} (24 \underline{\quad} 35) = 78$ b) $83 \underline{\quad} (76 \underline{\quad} 38) = 121$

   c) $14 \underline{\quad} (8 \underline{\quad} 3) = 70$ d) $56 \underline{\quad} (24 \underline{\quad} 6) = 14$

   e) $143 \underline{\quad} (36 \underline{\quad} 3) = 35$ f) $24 \underline{\quad} (76 \underline{\quad} 19) = 34656$

$$9 \_\_\_ 3 \_\_\_ 4 = 48$$

This time you have no brackets to help you, so what are the possibilities?

$$9 \_\_\_ (3 \_\_\_ 4) = 48$$

$$(9 \_\_\_ 3) \_\_\_ 4 = 48$$

One possibility will work and one will not.
But which is which? Work it out yourself.

4. Find the missing symbols.

a) $7 \_\_\_ 2 \_\_\_ 3 = 27$ b) $10 \_\_\_ 5 \_\_\_ 6 = 12$ c) $11 \_\_\_ 4 \_\_\_ 5 = 35$

d) $8 \_\_\_ 6 \_\_\_ 12 = 4$ e) $12 \_\_\_ 3 \_\_\_ 5 = 96$ f) $14 \_\_\_ 7 \_\_\_ 7 = 49$

g) $40 \_\_\_ 11 \_\_\_ 3 = 5$ h) $56 \_\_\_ 7 \_\_\_ 9 = 72$ i) $6 \_\_\_ 108 \_\_\_ 12 = 15$

5. Use your calculator to see if you can work out the missing symbols in these mathematical sentences.

a) $37 \_\_\_ 21 \_\_\_ 23 = 800$ b) $27 \_\_\_ 36 \_\_\_ 11 = 675$

c) $125 \_\_\_ 25 \_\_\_ 94 = 380$

Puzzler

Each letter is worth a number of points. Each letter must correspond to a different number, and no letter has the value of zero. The points are added up to make the total for the word. Try to work out the number of points for each letter and then find the value of the last word.

TEE = 4   TEN = 6
NEST = 10   TENTS = ?

How many points would TENTS get?

Number Patterns and Sequences

Look at this sequence of coloured squares. Can you spot a pattern? How would you describe the pattern? Discuss this with the people near you.

Now make patterns of your own in your copy. Ask your friends to describe the patterns you have created.

Now look at this sequence of numbers.

$$3, 4, 6, 9, 13, 18, 24$$

How would you describe the pattern of the numbers?

The first term of the sequence is ____.
To get the second term, you add ____.
The gap between each term after that increases by ____.

1. Look at these sequences of numbers. See if you can spot and describe the patterns.
   a) 1, 6, 4, 9, 7, 12, 10, 15
   b) 28, 21, 15, 10, 6, 3, 1
   c) 4, 6, 10, 16, 24, 34, 46
   d) 40, 29, 20, 13, 8, 5, 4
   e) $\frac{3}{4}$, $1\frac{1}{2}$, $2\frac{1}{4}$, 3, $3\frac{3}{4}$, $4\frac{1}{2}$
   f) $\frac{1}{6}$, $\frac{1}{3}$, $\frac{1}{2}$, $\frac{2}{3}$, $\frac{5}{6}$, 1
   g) 0.3, 0.7, 1.1, 1.5, 1.9, 2.3
   h) 3.2, 2.9, 3.6, 3.3, 4.0, 3.7

2. Now spot the pattern and then fill in the next 2 terms in each sequence.
   a) 17, 23, 29, 35, ____, ____
   b) 63, 54, 45, 36, ____, ____
   c) 5, 10, 20, 40, ____, ____
   d) 1, 3, 6, 10, 15, ____, ____
   e) 2.9, 3.6, 4.3, 5.0, ____, ____
   f) 0.1, $\frac{3}{10}$, 0.5, $\frac{7}{10}$, ____, ____

3. a) Can you make the pattern in your copy?

   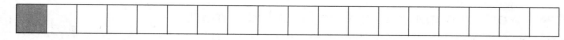

   - Colour the first square blue.
   - Colour the next 2 squares orange.
   - Colour the next 2 squares pink.
   - Colour the next square green.
   - Repeat the pattern.

   b) Make up your own list of instructions for a pattern of coloured squares. Try it out on the people near you.

4. Look at this list of instructions for making a number pattern.
    - Start with the number 7.
    - To find the next term, add 9.
    - Each new term is 9 more than the previous term.
    - There are 5 terms in the pattern: 7, 16, ____, ____, ____. Complete the pattern.

5. Now make these patterns.

    a) Start with the number 10. To find the next term, add 1. The difference between each new term increases by 1. There are 7 terms in the pattern.

    b) Start with the number 68. To find the next term, subtract 8. The difference between each new term decreases by 1. There are 5 terms in the pattern.

    c) Start with the second square number. To find the next term, multiply by 3. Each new term is 3 times bigger than the previous term. There are 6 terms in the pattern.

    d) Start with the square root of 9. To find the second term, add 5. To find the third term, subtract 2. To find the fourth term, add 5. To find the fifth term, subtract 2. Repeat the pattern. There are 9 terms in the pattern.

6. Look at this pattern carefully.

    7, 14, 21, 27, 35, 42, 49

    Each term in the pattern is a multiple of 7, except for one. Can you spot the odd one out?

7. Now pick the odd terms out in these number patterns.

    a) 2, 7, 12, 17, 21, 27

    b) 1, 4, 9, 15, 25, 36, 49

    c) 93, 81, 69, 57, 45, 34

    d) 128, 62, 32, 16, 8, 4, 2, 1

    e) 13, 26, 39, 42, 65

    f) 1, 5, 25, 125, 620, 3125

Cracking the Code

a = 1	b = 2	c = 3	d = 4	e = 5	f = 6
g = 7	h = 8	i = 9	j = 10	k = 11	l = 12
m = 13	n = 14	o = 15	p = 16	q = 17	r = 18
s = 19	t = 20	u = 21	v = 22	w = 23	x = 24
y = 25	z = 26				

As you can see, every letter in the alphabet has been given a number. This means that we can work out the number that any word represents by adding the value of the letters together.

So the word 'it' = i + t = 9 + 20 = 29.

8. Work out the value of these words.

   a) add   b) not   c) bin   d) make   e) code   f) maths

Puzzler

cat   ale   map   oat   gun   bead

You have to arrange these 6 words in the correct order to make up a number pattern. The number pattern is as follows:

Start with the number 12. To find the next term, add 6.
Each term in the sequence is 6 more than the previous term.
There are 6 terms in the sequence.

To work it out, make the number pattern first. Then use your code to work out the number that each word represents. Now match the numbers to the pattern and you have the sequence of the words.

Homework

1. Work these out.

   a) (48 + 37) × 15   b) 219 × (71 − 53)   c) 625 − (187 + 359)

   d) 147 ÷ (53 − 46)   e) 1274 + (347 × 6)   f) 3014 − (6254 − 4775)

2. Now try these.

   a) 68 × 18 + 1567   b) 207 + 864 ÷ 9   c) 6384 − 237 × 17

   d) 2531 + 4186 − 3749   e) 195 × 525 ÷ 7   f) 948 ÷ 6 + 548

3. Put the correct symbols into these.

a) $7 + (8 \_\_\_ 3) = 18$

b) $(3 \times 3) \_\_\_ 4 = 36$

c) $(12 - 7) \_\_\_ 8 = 13$

d) $72 \_\_\_ (64 \div 8) = 9$

e) $(6 \_\_\_ 8) - 9 = 39$

f) $96 \div (3 \_\_\_ 4) = 8$

4. Find the missing symbols.

a) $7 \_\_\_ 4 \_\_\_ 3 = 49$

b) $18 \_\_\_ 3 \_\_\_ 6 = 12$

c) $12 \_\_\_ 9 \_\_\_ 9 = 27$

d) $5 \_\_\_ 8 \_\_\_ 4 = 10$

e) $11 \_\_\_ 4 \_\_\_ 3 = 77$

f) $12 \_\_\_ 5 \_\_\_ 6 = 42$

5. Look at these sequences of numbers. See if you can spot and describe the patterns.

a) 1, 7, 10, 16, 19, 25, 28, 34

b) 32, 31, 29, 26, 22, 17, 11

c) 2, 4, 8, 16, 32, 64, 128

d) 160, 80, 40, 20, 10, 5

e) 0.4, 1.1, 1.8, 2.5, 3.2, 3.9

f) 9.3, 8.1, 6.9, 5.7, 4.5, 3.3

6. Now spot the pattern and then fill in the next 2 terms in each sequence.

a) 9, 16, 23, 30, ___, ___

b) 72, 64, 56, 48, ___, ___

c) 1, 3, 9, 27, ___, ___

d) 625, 125, 25, ___, ___

e) 6.9, 5.8, 4.7, ___, ___

f) 3.7, 6.1, 8.5, ___, ___

Recap

- I know whether to add, subtract, multiply or divide. ⭘⭘⭘

- I can recognise and describe number patterns. ⭘⭘⭘

- I can make number sequences. ⭘⭘⭘

- I can use a pattern to solve a problem. ⭘⭘⭘

 # Talk About

1. What units of measurement would you use to measure the following distances? Would it be kilometres and metres (km and m), metres and centimetres (m and cm) or centimetres and millimetres (cm and mm)?

   a) The distance between your house and the school

   b) The distance between your desk and the door of the classroom

   c) The distance travelled by a snail in 30 seconds

   d) The distance travelled by light in 1 second

   e) The distance you could throw a ball

   f) The distance you can stick out your tongue

2. Fill in the blanks in these sentences so that each of the sentences is accurate.

   a) There are ____ millimetres in a centimetre.

   b) A _____ is $\frac{1}{100}$ of a metre.

   c) A kilometre is made up of 1000 _____.

   d) There are ____ millimetres in a metre.

   e) There are 100000 _____ in a kilometre.

Millimetres and Centimetres

There are 10mm in 1cm, so:

0mm 10 20 30

$$1mm = \frac{1}{10}cm$$

Strand: Measures
Curriculum Objectives:
Select and use appropriate instruments of measurement;
rename measures of length;

estimate and measure the perimeter of regular and irregular shapes;
use and interpret scales on maps and plans

1. Write these millimetre amounts as fractions of a cm. Remember to reduce the fractions to their lowest terms.

   a) 3mm = _____cm

   b) 5mm = _____cm

   c) 2mm = _____cm

   d) 7mm = _____cm

   e) 8mm = _____cm

   f) 9mm = _____cm

   g) 11mm = _____cm

   h) 14mm = _____cm

   i) 26mm = _____cm

   j) 35mm = _____cm

   k) 48mm = _____cm

   l) 63mm = _____cm

   > If 1mm = $\frac{1}{10}$cm, then 1mm = 0._____cm.

2. Fill in the blanks.

   a) _____mm = 0.6cm

   b) 4mm = _____cm

   c) _____mm = 0.8cm

   d) 17mm = _____cm

   e) _____mm = 2.2cm

   f) 39mm = _____cm

   g) _____mm = 5cm

   h) 84mm = _____cm

Centimetres, Metres and Kilometres

> There are 100cm in a metre, so 1cm = $\frac{1}{100}$m = 0.01m.
>
> There are 1000m in a kilometre, so 1m = $\frac{1}{1000}$km = 0.001km

3. Use this information to fill in the spaces in this table.

Measurement	Fraction	Decimal
17cm		
		0.08m
	$\frac{39}{100}$m	
151cm		
	$2\frac{3}{4}$m	
		3.4m
328m		
	$1\frac{23}{1000}$km	
		2.125km
1005m		
		0.08km
	$2\frac{1}{5}$km	

Adding and Subtracting Lengths

1. Now try these. Remember to change the lengths so that they are all written in the same way before adding or subtracting. Record the unit of measurement in your answer.

   a) 37mm + 4cm 9mm + 6.5cm

   b) $5\frac{1}{2}$cm + 163mm + 8.4cm

   c) 9m 6cm + 179cm + 2.87m

   d) 3.79m + $1\frac{1}{4}$m + 705cm

   e) 235m + 1km 68m + 3.592km

   f) 1.83km + 2078m + $5\frac{1}{5}$km

   g) 10cm 3mm − 4.8cm

   h) $9\frac{4}{5}$cm − 8cm 9mm

   i) 5.35m − 3m 8cm

   j) 943cm − $7\frac{3}{4}$m

   k) 6592m − 2km 79m

   l) 1.258km − $\frac{5}{8}$km

2. On a cycling holiday a family cycled 18km 376m the first day, 16.267km the second day and $19\frac{3}{5}$km the third day. How far did they cycle in total?

3. At the start of the week, Paul's candy cane was 162mm long. After he had licked it several times a day, the candy cane was only 8.7cm long at the end of the week. How much shorter was the candy cane at the end of the week than it was at the beginning of the week?

Puzzler

A piece of paper is 23.6cm long. If you fold the piece of paper in half and then fold it in half again, how long is the piece of paper?

There is more than 1 answer to this question. How many answers can you find? Explain how you worked it out. It may help to try it with a piece of paper.

Multiplying and Dividing Lengths

> When multiplying or dividing lengths, you can choose which way you prefer to write the length, but remember to record the unit of measurement in your answer.

1. Work out how far each team ran in total in the All-Ireland Relay Championships.

Distance run by each runner	Number of runners	Total length run
1074m	7	
2km 47m	9	
35.72m	12	
1.836km	17	
28¾m	29	
2.039km	36	

2. Now work out how far each runner had to run in these relay races.

Distance run by the team	Number of runners	Distance run by each runner
1km 835m	5	
0.756km	9	
5670m	6	
1.566km	27	
1⅞km	25	
2km 90m	38	

3. A toddler built a tower of bricks. If he used 7 bricks that were each 4cm 3mm tall and 9 bricks that were each 3.8cm tall, how tall was the tower?

4. The feared pirate Short Bob Copper buried his booty on a desert island so that nobody except him could ever find it. He used a rock as a marker. From the rock he took 9 paces north, 8 paces west and then a further 7 paces north. If each of his paces was 0.84m, what distance did he walk from the rock?

5. Bob's twin brother, Equally Short Bill Copper, was also in the piracy business. As luck would have it, he also chose to bury his booty on an island. He used a tree as a marker and walked 12 paces south and 6 paces east. However, Bill had a wooden leg and as a result his paces were shorter than his brother's. If the treasure was a distance of 13.68m from the tree, how long was each of Bill's paces?

Perimeter

1. Choose the correct answer. Perimeter is:
   a) The measure of the space contained inside a shape
   b) The measure of the space outside a shape
   c) The measure of the total length of the sides of a shape

2. Mr Baker the baker made some unusually shaped birthday cakes and now he doesn't know what length of ribbon he needs to tie around each of the cakes. Can you help him? He needs to find the perimeter of each of the cakes and he needs an extra 13cm per cake to tie the ribbon.

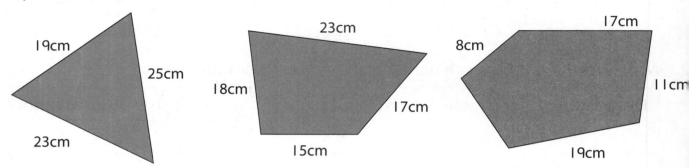

Puzzler

Do you remember what a regular polygon is? Is it:
a) A shape that has the same number of sides as angles?
b) A shape whose sides are of equal length?
c) A shape that has more than 4 sides?

(Hint: a square is a regular polygon.)

> If we know the length of a side of a regular polygon, what would be a quick way of working out the perimeter?

3. Find the perimeters of these regular polygons.

Shape	Length of side	Number of sides	Perimeter
Square	28.6cm		
Octagon	7.37m		
Pentagon	35.2cm		
Decagon	4m 6cm		
Equilateral triangle	436mm		
Heptagon	9cm 8mm		
Nonagon	2.83m		
Hexagon	8m 24cm		

Scale

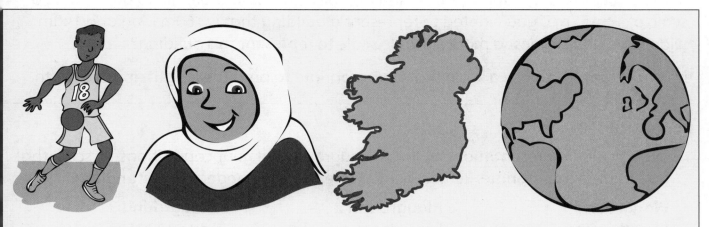

Look at the pictures above. Are all the pictures the same size? Are all the pictures the same size in real life? How do you make them the same size in the pictures?

Task:

Draw an accurate picture/representation of the table you are sitting at, assuming that it is 90cm long and 60m wide.

There are 2 ways of doing this.

● The first way requires you to get your hands on an enormous piece of paper.
● The second way requires you to find a way of representing the table but on a smaller **scale**. (To scale something down means to make it smaller.)

If we were to let 1cm represent 10cm of the table, we could fit it comfortably on a page in your copy. So if 10cm is represented by 1cm, how long and how wide would your drawing of the table be? Draw the scaled-down picture of the table in your copy.

The scale of the drawing is 1cm : 10cm.

Write the scale under your drawing. Why is this important?

You can draw much bigger shapes to scale.

1. Draw these rectangular-shaped schoolyards into your copy using the scale 1cm : 4m.

Schoolyard 1
Length – 32m
Width – 16m

Schoolyard 2
Length – 36m
Width – 48m

Schoolyard 3
Length – 28m
Width – 24m

Schoolyard 4
Length – 44m
Width – 20m

Schoolyard 5
Length – 18m
Width – 12m

Schoolyard 6
Length – 30m
Width – 26m

Some scales are more appropriate than others. Why would there be no point using a scale of 1cm : 2m if you wanted to represent a building that is 160m long and 140m wide? Can you suggest a more suitable scale to represent this building?

It's important to choose a scale that is appropriate to both the length and the width.

2. Draw scaled representations of these playgrounds in your copy. Choose a scale that you think is appropriate. Remember to write the scale under the rectangles.

Playground 1
Length – 27m
Width – 21m

Playground 2
Length – 18m
Width – 12m

Playground 3
Length – 35m
Width – 28m

Playground 4
Length – 60m
Width – 50m

Playground 5
Length – 88m
Width – 32m

Playground 6
Length – 54m
Width – 45m

Farmer Ted is planning to put a fence around his field. To plan it properly, he needs to know the exact length and width of his field. This is a scaled picture of his field.

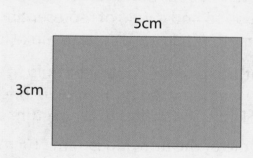

5cm

3cm

Scale 1cm : 4.9m

What is the actual length and width of this field?

Length = 5cm   Scale = 1cm : 4.9m   Actual length = 5 × 4.9m = ?
Width = 3cm   Scale = 1cm : 4.9m   Actual width = 3 × 4.9m = ?

3. Now work out the actual lengths and widths of these fields.

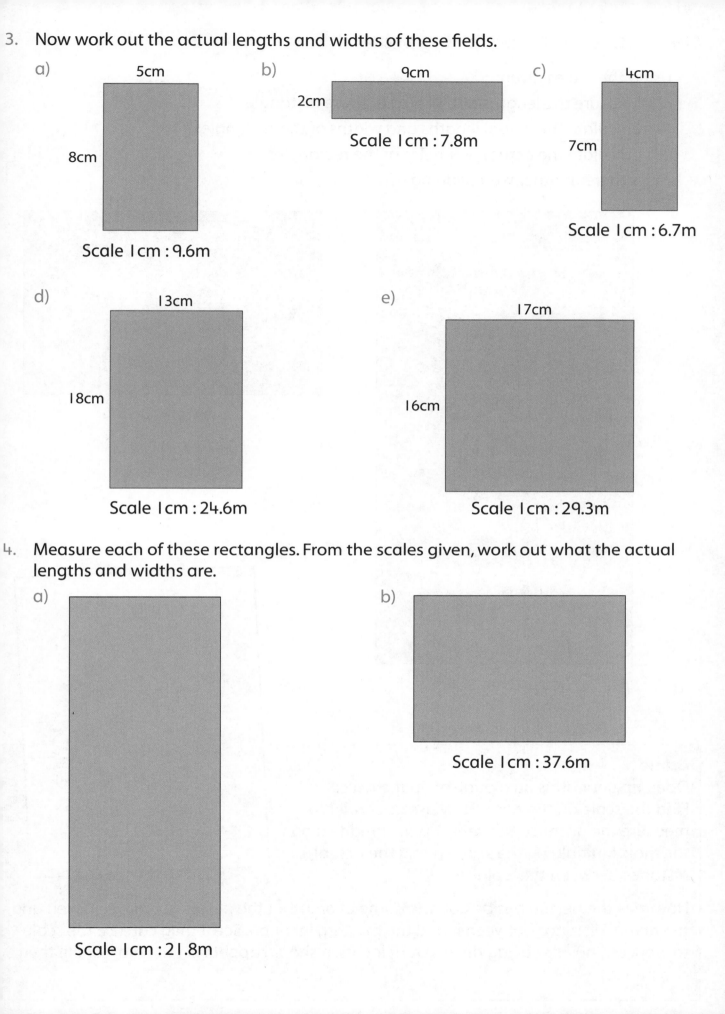

a)
5cm

8cm

Scale 1cm : 9.6m

b)
9cm

2cm

Scale 1cm : 7.8m

c)
4cm

7cm

Scale 1cm : 6.7m

d)
13cm

18cm

Scale 1cm : 24.6m

e)
17cm

16cm

Scale 1cm : 29.3m

4. Measure each of these rectangles. From the scales given, work out what the actual lengths and widths are.

a)

Scale 1cm : 21.8m

b)

Scale 1cm : 37.6m

Calculating Perimeter Using Scale

1. Using the scales given:
   a) Measure the lengths and widths of these rectangles
   b) Calculate the actual lengths and widths of the rectangles
   c) Calculate the actual perimeter of the rectangles
   d) Is there another way of doing it?

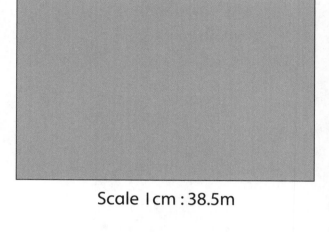

Scale 1cm : 38.5m

Scale 1cm : 31.6m

Game

Open up your atlas on a page of your choice. Find the scale on the page. Now use your ruler to measure the distance between 2 places marked on the map. Multiply by the scale to find the actual distance between the 2 places.

Now give the person beside you the name of only 1 of the places you have chosen and the actual distance between it and the mystery location. See if they can use the scale to work out how far away the mystery location should appear on the map and if they can find it.

Can you think of a piece of mathematical equipment that might be useful in finding the mystery location?

Can you think of other games you could play using your atlas and scale? Discuss it with the people near you.

While warming up for PE, the teacher asked her 6th class to do a lap of the outside of the PE hall, but nobody knew how far they had to run. One bright spark suggested they could work it out by looking at the plans of the school buildings. This is the plan.

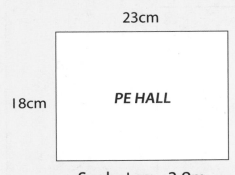

23cm

18cm

PE HALL

Scale 1cm : 3.9m

What is the perimeter of the PE hall?

There are a couple of ways of working out the actual perimeter. You could work out the perimeter of the scaled-down drawing and then multiply by the scale, or you could work out the actual length and the actual width and work out the perimeter from there. Try both ways and see which way you find easier.

Option 1
(23 + 18) × 2 = perimeter
perimeter × 3.9m = actual perimeter

Option 2
23 × 3.9m = actual length
18 × 3.9m = actual width

(actual length + actual width) × 2 = actual perimeter

2. Work out the perimeters of these other schoolrooms that were also shown in the plans.

Room	Length	Width	Scale	Perimeter
Junior Infants	3cm	4cm	1cm : 3.9m	
Senior Infants	3.7cm	3.3cm	1cm : 3.9m	
1st Class	2.8cm	4.5cm	1cm : 3.9m	
2nd Class	3.4cm	4.2cm	1cm : 3.9m	
3rd Class	3.9cm	4.4cm	1cm : 3.9m	
4th Class	4.1cm	4.1cm	1cm : 3.9m	
5th Class	4.2cm	3.8cm	1cm : 3.9m	
6th Class	4cm	4.6cm	1cm : 3.9m	
Office	1.8cm	2.3cm	1cm : 3.9m	

3. Work out the actual perimeter of this house from the plans.

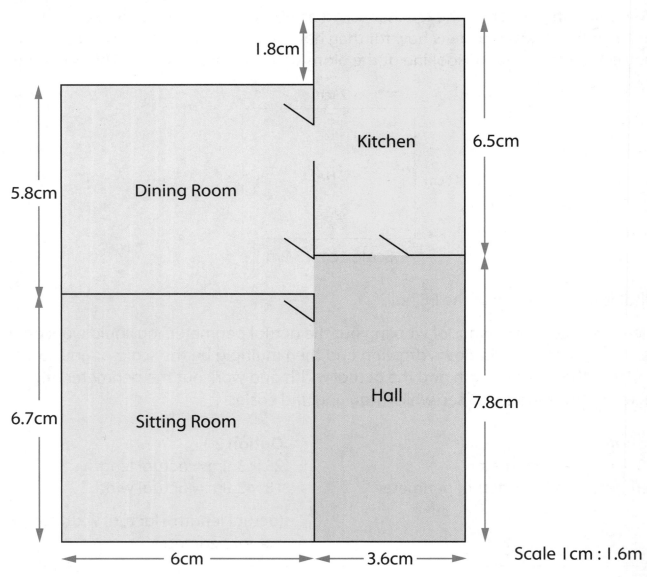

Scale 1cm : 1.6m

Homework

1. Try these. Remember to change the lengths so that they are all written in the same way before adding. Record the unit of measurement in your answer.

   a) 3.8cm + 2cm 6mm + 49mm

   b) 7.4cm + 98mm + 11cm 7mm

   c) 1.85m + 207cm + 4m 36cm

   d) 345cm + $3\frac{3}{4}$m + 6m 68cm

   e) $7\frac{2}{5}$km + 4km 83m + 5.274km

   f) 3.09km + 4835m + 5km 628m

2. Now try these.

   a) 125mm − 3.9cm

   b) 7cm 2mm − $3\frac{3}{5}$cm

   c) 6m 8cm − 176cm

   d) $8\frac{3}{10}$m − 4.79m

   e) 8.38km − 1986m

   f) 7km 25m − 5.174km

3. Multiply these lengths and record the units of measurement in your answers.

   a) 13.8cm × 9

   b) 9cm 6mm × 27

   c) 2m 76cm × 14

   d) 458cm × 34

   e) 7km 87m × 18

   f) 4km 154m × 46

4. Divide these lengths and record the units of measurement in your answers.

   a) 63cm 2mm ÷ 8

   b) 59.2cm ÷ 16

   c) 16m 32cm ÷ 24

   d) 14.7m ÷ 35

   e) 6km 25m ÷ 25

   f) 9.614km ÷ 38

5. What is the perimeter of each of the following shapes?

   a) A square with sides measuring 18cm

   b) A hexagon with sides measuring 29cm

   c) An equilateral triangle with sides measuring 47cm

   d) An octagon with sides measuring 36cm

6. Draw these rectangular-shaped fields in your copy using the scale 1cm : 5m.

   Field 1
   Length − 25m
   Width − 15m

   Field 2
   Length − 40m
   Width − 35m

   Field 3
   Length − 45m
   Width − 20m

   Field 4
   Length − 45m
   Width − 20m

   Field 5
   Length − 55m
   Width − 30m

   Field 6
   Length − 50m
   Width − 15m

7. Draw scaled representations of these fields in your copy. Choose a scale that you think is appropriate. Remember to write the scale under the rectangles.

Field 1
Length – 24m
Width – 16m

Field 2
Length – 27m
Width – 18m

Field 3
Length – 36m
Width – 24m

Field 4
Length – 32m
Width – 24m

Field 5
Length – 45m
Width – 27m

Field 6
Length – 44m
Width – 33m

8. Work out the perimeter of the following rectangles.

Rectangle 1
Length – 6cm
Width – 5cm
Scale – 1cm : 7cm

Rectangle 2
Length – 12cm
Width – 7cm
Scale – 1cm : 14cm

Rectangle 3
Length – 4.7cm
Width – 2.6cm
Scale 1cm : 3.8m

Rectangle 4
Length – 3.9cm
Width – 1.8cm
Scale – 1cm : 5.2m

Rectangle 5
Length – 4.3cm
Width – 2.7cm
Scale – 1cm : 26.1m

Rectangle 6
Length – 5.4cm
Width – 1.6cm
Scale – 1cm : 32.7m

Recap

- I can choose appropriate units of measurement. ○ ○ ○

- I can add and subtract lengths recorded in different ways. ○ ○ ○

- I can multiply and divide lengths recorded in different ways. ○ ○ ○

- I know what perimeter is. ○ ○ ○

- I can use scale to calculate actual dimensions. ○ ○ ○

- I can calculate perimeter using scale. ○ ○ ○

Talk About

Think of your kitchen at home. It's probably full of 3-D shapes. List 10 things in the kitchen that are particular 3-D shapes. Here are the names of some 3-D shapes to help you.

sphere

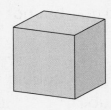

cube

cone

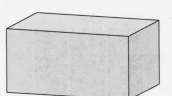

cuboid

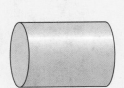

cylinder

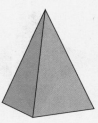

pyramid

No.	Object	Shape
1		
2		
3		
4		
5		
6		
7		
8		
9		
10		

In fact, 3-D shapes are all around us. See if you can spot some either inside or outside the classroom. Explore the school and see who can discover the most interesting examples of well-known 3-D shapes. Compare your findings when you get back to the classroom.

Strand: Shape and Space
Curriculum Objectives:
Identify and examine 3-D shapes and explore relationships, including octahedron (faces, edges and vertices);

1. a) An ice-cream cone is made up of a combination of two 3-D shapes. Can you tell what they are from looking at the picture?

   b) Make a list of other objects that are made up of combinations of 3-D shapes.

Nets of 3-D Shapes

> A **net** is a 3-D shape that is waiting to be assembled.

2. a) Study the following nets and see if you can spot which 3-D shape they make. Here's a list of shapes to help you, but not every shape on the list has a matching net below.

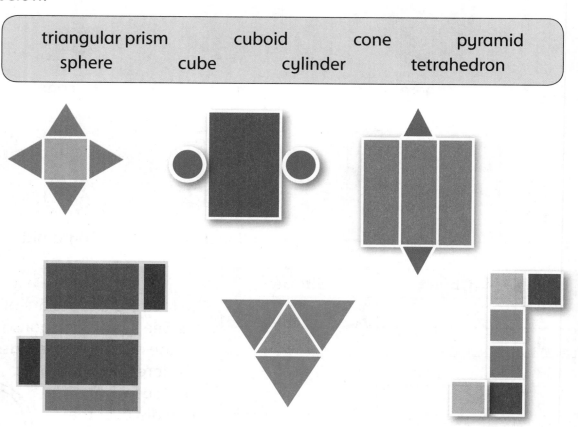

   triangular prism   cuboid   cone   pyramid
   sphere   cube   cylinder   tetrahedron

   b) Now draw the nets onto different pieces of paper. Cut them out and assemble them into their 3-D shapes to see if you were right.

Puzzler

There is one 3-D shape that has no net. Can you guess which one it is? Discuss it with the people near you and see if you can agree on an answer. Why does it not have a net?

Properties of 3-D Shapes

3-D shapes can be sorted into 2 categories: 3-D shapes that have only flat surfaces and 3-D shapes that have curved surfaces.

1. Sort the shapes in the list on the previous page into these 2 categories.

3-D shapes with flat surfaces only	3-D shapes with curved surfaces

2. a) A 3-D shape that only has flat surfaces is called a poly_____.
   (Hint: the answer is not pocket!)

   b) A 3-D shape that only has flat surfaces and whose flat surfaces are exactly the same shape and size is called a reg_____ poly_____.

3. Now sort your list of shapes with flat surfaces only.

Poly_____	Reg_____ poly_____

4. Look at this diagram of a cube. Can you label the parts the arrows are pointing to?

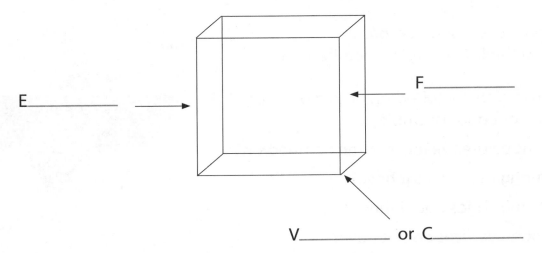

E_____

F_____

V_____ or C_____

Let's take a closer look at a cube.

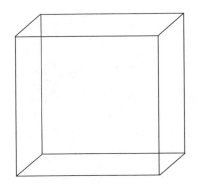

a) How many faces does it have?

b) Are all the faces flat?

c) What does this make it?

d) Are all the faces exactly the same size and shape?

e) What does this mean?

f) How many edges does the cube have?

g) How many corners (vertices) does the cube have?

5. Use the nets you have made or any shapes you have in the classroom to fill in the spaces in this table.

	No. of faces	Edges	Vertices	Polyhedron (yes/no)	Regular polyhedron (yes/no)
Cuboid					
Cylinder					
Pyramid					
Cone					
Tetrahedron					
Sphere					
Triangular prism					
Cube					
Pentagonal prism					

6. This is the net of an octahedron.
   Why do you think it's called an octahedron?

7. Copy the net of the octahedron onto a piece of paper. Cut it out and assemble it.

   a) What shape are the faces of the octahedron?

   b) How many faces does it have?

   c) How many edges does it have?

   d) How many vertices does it have?

   e) Is it a regular polyhedron?

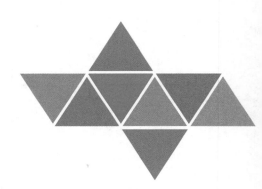

Homework

1. Draw nets for the following 3-D shapes.

   cube   pyramid   cylinder   cuboid   tetrahedron

2. Draw 3 different types of net for a cuboid.

3. On this cuboid, label a face, an edge and a vertex.

4. Name that shape!

a) I have 6 faces. All of my faces are flat. All of my edges are the same.

b) I have 3 faces. 2 of them are flat and 1 of them is curved.

c) I have 5 faces. 4 of them are triangles and 1 of them is a square.

d) I have 5 faces. 2 of them are triangles and the other 3 are rectangles.

e) I have 4 faces and all of them are triangles.

5. If this Rubik's cube was painted completely white and the cube was then dismantled into the 27 individual smaller cubes, how many of those cubes would have 2 faces painted white?

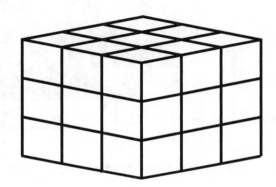

Talk About

1. Have a look at the picture and find some special offers that use percentages. Can you make up 3 of your own special offers using percentages?

Remember:
the word *per cent* means *for each hundred.*

Oranges 10% extra free when you buy 10 or more

Apples 20% off

Grapes 5% off per bunch

2. Find 5 words that contain the word *cent* and explain the meaning of each.

3. What percentage of each of these 100-squares is
   a) green
   b) pink and
   c) white?

Strand: Number
Curriculum Objectives:
Use percentages and relate them to fractions and decimals;
compare and order percentages of numbers;
solve problems relating to profit and loss, discount VAT interest increases decreases

Fractions, Decimals and Percentages

Like fractions and decimals, we use per cent to describe a proportion or a quantity.
For example: in a test, Colm got 82 out of 100 questions right.
We can write this as $\frac{82}{100}$, 0.82 or 82%.

1. Express these fractions as percentages:
   a) $\frac{27}{100}$ b) $\frac{3}{100}$ c) $\frac{42}{100}$ d) $\frac{16}{100}$ e) $\frac{31}{100}$ f) $\frac{9}{100}$

   g) $\frac{88}{100}$ h) $\frac{65}{100}$ i) $\frac{71}{100}$ j) $\frac{94}{100}$ k) $\frac{12}{100}$ l) $\frac{100}{100}$

2. There are 100 children in each school. From the information given in the table, can you work out the percentages of boys and girls in each school?

Number of girls	Fraction of girls	Percentage of girls	Number of boys	Fraction of boys	Percentage of boys	Total children
62	$\frac{62}{100}$		38			100
76			24	$\frac{24}{100}$		100
38						100
			71			100
56						100

Fractions are not always written as hundredths, so before we change them to percentages, we need to write them as equivalent fractions with a denominator of 100.

$$\frac{1}{5} = \frac{1}{5} \times \frac{20}{20} = \frac{20}{100} = 20\%$$

3. Convert the fractions to hundredths and then percentages.
   a) $\frac{1}{2} = \frac{}{100} = $ ____%   b) $\frac{7}{10}$ c) $\frac{2}{5}$ d) $\frac{1}{4}$ e) $\frac{3}{4}$ f) $\frac{3}{10}$

4. What percentage of each of theses shapes is a) pink b) white?
   (Hint: write your answers as fractions first.)

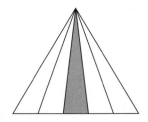
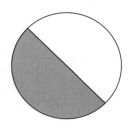
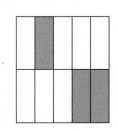
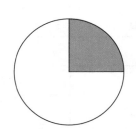
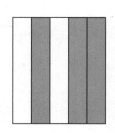

It's not always possible to change the given fractions to equivalent fractions with a denominator of 100. For example:

Write $\frac{1}{8}$ as a percentage.

We can do this in 2 ways:

$$\frac{1}{8} \text{ of } 100\% = \frac{1}{8} \times \frac{100}{1} = \frac{25}{2}\% = 12\frac{1}{2}\%$$

or

Change to decimal: 8 ⟌ 1.000

$$0.125 = 12.5\% \text{ or } 12\frac{1}{2}\%$$

5. Write these fractions as percentages using one of the methods above.

   a) $\frac{1}{3}$ b) $\frac{3}{8}$ c) $\frac{2}{3}$ d) $\frac{5}{8}$

6. Write these percentages as fractions in their lowest terms.

   a) $75\% = \frac{}{100} = \frac{}{4}$ b) 10% c) 50%

   d) 35% e) 82% f) 63%

   g) 90% h) 15% i) 2%

7. Change these decimals to fractions and then percentages.

   a) $0.61 = \frac{}{100} = $ ____% b) 0.39 c) 0.04

   d) 0.92 e) 0.15 f) 0.56

   g) 0.28 h) 0.64 i) 0.01

8. Complete this table.

Decimal	Fraction	Percentage
0.5		
		17%
	$\frac{9}{10}$	
0.48		
		25%
	$\frac{41}{100}$	
0.26		
		40%
	$\frac{4}{5}$	
0.85		

Calculating Percentages

1.

Who ate more?

James ate 45% of a pizza

Colin ate $\frac{2}{5}$ of a pizza

2.

Who read more?

Rebecca read 72% of a book

Leanne read 0.75 of a book

3.

In tennis, who had more first serves inside the line?

David got $\frac{8}{10}$ of his serves in. Liam got 82% of his serves in

4. Find the percentage.

a) Brian drank 38% of his carton of juice during his break time. What percentage of the carton was left to drink with his lunch?

b) Niamh used 56% of her mobile phone credit over the weekend and will not be getting more credit until next weekend. What percentage of her phone credit does she have left for the week?

25% of the class are over 12 years old. If there are 32 children in the class, how many are over 12?

This problem can be solved in 2 ways:

Fraction method

$25\% = \frac{25}{100} = \frac{1}{4}$

$\frac{1}{4}$ of 32 = 32 ÷ 4 = 8

So there are 8 children over 12.

Decimal method

$25\% = 0.25$

0.25 of 32 = 0.25 × 32 = 8.00

So there are 8 children over 12.

Find what percentage of your class are over 12.

5. Use one of the methods above to find:

a) 50% of 108

b) 20% of 640

c) 32% of 500

d) 40% of 160

e) 75% of 360

f) 10% of 850

g) 5% of 200

h) 28% of 400

i) 25% of 12

j) 90% of 760

k) 2% of 1000

l) 65% of 140

Chocolate Brownies

6. a) The total weight of the ingredients is 1000g (or 1kg). Work out how many grams of each ingredient are needed.

   25% margarine
   35% brown sugar
   5% cocoa powder
   $27\frac{1}{2}$% self-raising flour
   $7\frac{1}{2}$% chocolate chips

   b) Find or invent 2 of your own percentage recipes. (Remember: total ingredients = 100%.)

7. The following people are travelling to different places in the country today. Work out how many kilometres each has travelled already and place them in order, starting with the person who has travelled the furthest.

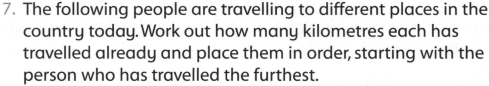

   Alison 30% of 210km   Alan 65% of 180km
   Philip 20% of 400km   Lucy 42% of 250km
   Mary 85% of 140km   Damien 18% of 450km

8. Barbara had €2.80 and spent 40% of her money on a book. How much money has she left?

9. A local concert hall has 850 seats. If 76% of the hall was filled at a concert last weekend, how many seats were occupied and how many seats were empty?

10. Susan got 85% correct on a recent test of 20 questions. How many questions did she get right?

Percentage Power

11. a) Find 65% of 500 on your calculator using only these keys:

$$500 \times 65\%$$

   b) Find 15% of 70 using only these keys:

$$70 \times 15\%$$

Define a rule for finding percentages with a calculator.

---

12. Now try these using your calculator.

   a) 68% of 50   b) 12% of 460   c) 10% of 760

   d) 24% of 1200   e) 55% of 830   f) 91% of 1700

   g) 15% of 650   h) 60% of 9400   i) 87% of 7690

   j) 70% of 30   k) 2% of 870   l) 49% of 1850

Writing One Number as a Percentage of Another

Out of a class of 30 children, 3 were absent on Friday. What percentage of the class was absent?

We can write this as a fraction: $\frac{3}{30}$ or $\frac{1}{10}$. We can then change this to a percentage in 2 ways.

Fraction method:

1. $\frac{1}{10}$ of $100\% = \frac{1}{10} \times \frac{100}{1} = \frac{100}{10} = 10\%$

2. $\frac{\overset{1}{3}}{\underset{10}{30}} \times \frac{100}{1} = \frac{100}{10} = 10\%$

Decimal method:

$$10 \overline{)1.00}$$
$$0.10 = 10\%$$

---

1. Write the following as percentages.

   a) 4 out of 20
   b) 50 out of 200
   c) 18 out of 30
   d) 48 out of 75
   e) 120 out of 160
   f) 210 out of 500
   g) 63 out of 90
   h) 77 out of 100
   i) 5 out of 40
   j) 35 out of 80
   k) 52 out of 65
   l) 150 out of 600

2. What percentage of each of these shapes are a) red b) blue c) yellow?

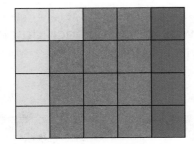  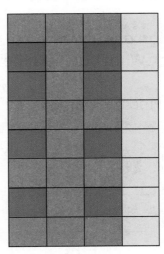

3. Jill had 48 colouring pencils but lost 6 of them. What percentage of the pencils did she lose?

4. Kevin has to draw a line measuring 50cm, but as his ruler is only 30cm long he has only drawn 30cm so far. What percentage of the line has he drawn?

5. Melissa is running a long-distance race of 5km. She has run 1.5km already.

   a) What percentage of the race has she run?

   b) What percentage of the race does she have left to run?

6. Survey the people in your class to find out:
   a) What percentage walk to school?
   b) What percentage are the eldest in their families?
   c) What percentage play a musical instrument?
   d) What percentage have pets at home?

Puzzler

If the number of pupils in a school increased from 240 to 300 one year and then back to 240 the following year, is it true to say that the percentage increase from year 1 to year 2 was the same as the percentage decrease from year 2 to year 3? Prove your answer.

7. a) What percentage of the European Union countries use the euro as their currency?
   b) What percentage do not use the euro?

8. What percentage of the Irish counties begins with the letter W?

9. Calculate what percentage of your family are over 20 years old.

10. Design a table to record what percentage of your class was in school each day last week. What day had the highest percentage of children in school?

11. a) Find the percentages.

Subject	Result	Out of	Percentage
English	42	50	
Gaeilge	60	75	
Maths	18	20	
Geography	132	150	

   b) Find some recent test results of your own and change them to percentages.

Increasing an Amount by a Percentage

1. During a promotion, a manufacturer decided to add 25% extra free to the following items. Calculate the total amount of each product now.

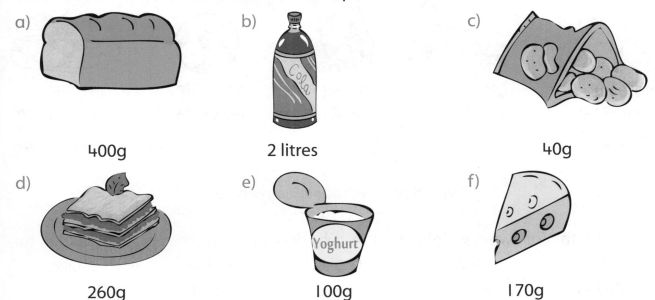

a) 400g

b) 2 litres

c) 40g

d) 260g

e) 100g

f) 170g

2. A computer store decided to increase its computer prices by 5%. Calculate the new price of each computer. The first one is done for you.

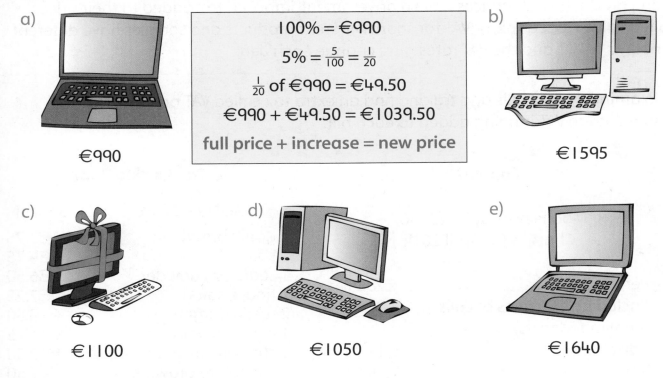

a) €990

$$100\% = €990$$
$$5\% = \frac{5}{100} = \frac{1}{20}$$
$$\frac{1}{20} \text{ of } €990 = €49.50$$
$$€990 + €49.50 = €1039.50$$
full price + increase = new price

b) €1595

c) €1100

d) €1050

e) €1640

3. Increase these lengths by 30%.

   a) 100m   b) 62m   c) 200m   d) 12m   e) 520m
   f) 782m   g) 118m   h) 1.6km   i) 2.78km

4. In January, an office worker received a 4% raise in his salary. If he earned a gross salary of €35000 last year, what is his new salary?

Decreasing an Amount by a Percentage

1. Super Sports Store is having an end of season sale. Calculate the sale price of each item.
   (Remember: in a sale, the price should be lower.)

15% off
Was €195

Now _____

10% off
Was €85

Now _____

25% off
Was €135

Now _____

33⅓% off
Was €36

Now _____

30% off
Was €69.50

Now _____

> **full price – decrease = new price**

2. Decrease the following weights by 15%. Check your answers using your calculator.
   a) 1.5kg   b) 2.68kg   c) 72.5kg   d) 0.6kg   e) 15.92kg
   f) 20.08kg   g) 46.4kg   h) 3.46kg   i) 128.2kg

VAT

Many products and services have a government-imposed tax added to their prices, called Value Added Tax, or VAT for short. Different products and services have different amounts of VAT and the VAT rates may change each year.

3. Examine these 2 bills and try and find an extra tax called VAT on them. What percentage VAT is being added to each bill?

Fone4U

Mobile no. – 082 1234567
Charges for April 2014

Perfect Package	€28.27
(including 100 mins of calls + unlimited texts)	
Call charges	€11.73
VAT	€ 5.00

****

AMOUNT DUE	€45.00

The Prickly Pear

Table No – 27 Waitress – Jennifer

1 garlic bread	€3.75
1 soup	€4.75
1 seafood chowder	€6.50
1 house salad	€7.25
2 rustic burgers	€19.50
1 pizza diavalo	€11.75
1 chicken curry	€10.50
2 chocolate brownies	€11.50
2 raspberry roulades	€14.50
1 fizzy water	€2.75
2 colas	€5.50
1 white wine	€4.75
VAT	€21.63

****

Total bill	€124.63

What is the total cost of a digital camera priced at €650 + VAT @ 21%?

We must find how much the VAT is by finding 21% of €650 and then adding it to the basic price:

21% of 650 = $\frac{21}{100}$ of €650 = 136.50   OR   21% of €650 = 0.21 × €650 = €136.50

€650 + €136.50 = total price = €786.50   €650 + €136.50 = total price = €786.50

+. Calculate a total restaurant bill of €124 plus 12.5% VAT.

5. A painter is painting the Walshs' house for €1450 plus VAT @ $12\frac{1}{2}$%. How much will the Walsh family have to pay in total?

6. The VAT on each of these items is 21%. Find the total price, including VAT, for each.

 €375    €65    €500    €45

Making a Profit

Shopkeepers and people in business buy products from a supplier at **cost price** and sell them at a higher **selling price** so that they will make a **profit**. How much profit they make depends on the percentage of the cost price they add on.

A shopkeeper bought a bed for €350 and sold it for €420. What profit did the shopkeeper make?

€350 = cost price
€420 = selling price
profit = selling price − cost price = €70

What was the percentage profit? We need to write the profit as a fraction of the cost price:

$$\frac{70}{350} = \frac{1}{5} \text{ and } \frac{1}{5} \text{ of } 100\% = 20\%$$

So the shopkeeper made a profit of €70, or 20%.

1. Work out the profit and the percentage profit for each of these.

	Cost price	Selling price	Profit	Percentage profit
Television	€200	€250		
Stereo	€125	€155		
DVD player	€160	€220		
MP3 player	€95	€133		
CD	€9	€13.50		
DVD	€15	€24		

2. A clothes shop bought a variety of clothes from a supplier and wants to add a 20% profit to each item. Help them work out the selling prices.

Cost price: €28   Cost price: €45   Cost price: €22   Cost price: €62

Selling price: _____   Selling price: _____   Selling price: _____   Selling price: _____

 Remember: cost price + profit = selling price

3. A car dealer bought a car for €12000 and sold it for €15000. Find the percentage profit.

4. A shopkeeper bought milk at 70c per litre. What price must it be sold at to make a profit of 15%?

Percentage Loss

Sometimes people have to sell items for less than they bought them. When this happens, a **loss** is made. The percentage loss is then subtracted from the cost price to find the selling price.

Helen bought a car for €18000 and sold it 2 years later for €15300.

a) What was the loss made on the car?

$$€18000 = \text{cost price}$$
$$€15300 = \text{selling price}$$
$$\text{loss} = \text{cost price} - \text{selling price} = €2700$$

b) Calculate the percentage loss on the car.

We need to write the loss as a fraction of the cost price:

$$\frac{2700}{18000} = \frac{3}{20} \text{ and } \frac{3}{20} \text{ as } \% = 15\%$$

1. Find the loss and the percentage loss of each of these.

	Bicycle	Motorbike	Scooter	Car	Van
Cost price	€240	€3500	€2900	€15000	€24000
Selling price	€160	€2800	€2030	€11250	€14400

2. Calculate the selling price for each of these.
   a) A bracelet bought for €25 and sold at a loss of 20%
   b) A violin bought for €750 and sold at a loss of 46%
   c) A kitchen table bought for €225 and sold at a loss of 16%
   d) A pair of rollerblades bought for €120 and sold at loss of 15%

3. A supermarket bought wine at a cost of €6 per bottle but had to sell it at €4.50 per bottle, as the labels were damaged. Calculate the percentage loss per bottle.

4. Calculate the percentage profit *or* loss made on each of these items.
   a) A dining room suite bought for €1200 and sold for €960
   b) A TV bought for €600 and sold for €732
   c) A washing machine bought for €320 and sold for €224
   d) A boat bought for €21000 and sold for €26460

Homework

1. Express these fractions as percentages.
   a) $\frac{49}{100}$ b) $\frac{8}{100}$ c) $\frac{27}{100}$ d) $\frac{13}{100}$ e) $\frac{38}{100}$

   f) $\frac{73}{100}$ g) $\frac{89}{100}$ h) $\frac{67}{100}$ i) $\frac{55}{100}$

2. Convert the fractions to hundredths and then percentages.
   a) $\frac{3}{5} = \frac{}{100} = \underline{\quad}\%$ b) $\frac{9}{10}$ c) $\frac{3}{4}$ d) $\frac{4}{5}$ e) $\frac{6}{10}$ f) $\frac{7}{20}$

3. Write these percentages as fractions in their lowest terms.

   a) $40\% = \dfrac{}{100} = \dfrac{}{5}$
   b) 70%
   c) 15%

   d) 36%
   e) 85%
   f) 56%

   g) 74%
   h) 95%
   i) 14%

4. Change these decimals to fractions and then percentages.

   a) $0.59 = \dfrac{}{100} = $ ___ %
   b) 0.23
   c) 0.84

   d) 0.05
   e) 0.37
   f) 0.18

   g) 0.44
   h) 0.65
   i) 0.99

5. Find:

   a) 10% of 190
   b) 25% of 184
   c) 20% of 225

   d) 40% of 345
   e) 75% of 296
   f) 30% of 780

   g) 15% of 340
   h) 85% of 980
   i) 16% of 125

6. Write the following as percentages.

   a) 7 out of 10
   b) 2 out of 5
   c) 9 out of 20

   d) 36 out of 40
   e) 140 out of 200
   f) 21 out of 28

   g) 72 out of 96
   h) 15 out of 25
   i) 8 out of 32

7. Increase these amounts by 40%.

   a) €160
   b) €185
   c) €220

   d) €265
   e) €310
   f) €1005

8. Decrease these amounts by 35%.

   a) €220
   b) €380
   c) €460

   d) €540
   e) €700
   f) €1060

9. Work out the profit and the percentage profit for each of these.

	Cost price	Selling price	Profit	Percentage profit
Laptop	€400	€440		
Printer	€140	€182		
Football boots	€48	€60		
Fridge	€300	€420		
Microwave	€64	€80		
Toaster	€15	€22.50		

0. Work out the loss and the percentage loss for each of these.

	Cost price	Selling price	Loss	Percentage loss
Bicycle	€160	€120		
Scooter	€70	€56		
Games console	€240	€192		
Rollerblades	€68	€51		
Cooker	€1080	€972		
Mobile phone	€60	€48		

1. Calculate the percentage profit *or* loss made on each of these items.

a) A computer bought for €640 and sold for €512

b) A car bought for €9600 and sold for €7200

c) A painting bought for €400 and sold for €520

d) An antique bought for €7000 and sold for €9800

Talk About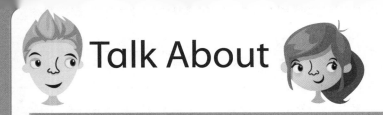

Puzzler

If Tony has an average score of 78% for the 4 maths tests he has completed so far, what is the lowest possible score he could have achieved on 1 test?

How many hours do you sleep at night? People sleep on average 8 hours a night. Does this mean that everyone sleeps for 8 hours? So what do you think average means?

If you described somebody as being above average or below average height, what would that mean?

See if you can find out what the average height is for men and women in Ireland. Is it different in other countries?

Estimating and Calculating Averages

How would you find the average weight of 5 children who were measured as follows?

41kg, 46kg, 36kg, 38kg, 44kg

41 + 46 + 36 + 38 + 44 = 205kg

$$5 \overline{)205}$$

41kg = average weight

1. Find the average of each of these. Estimate your answer first.

   a) 4, 7, 9, 11, 14

   b) 76c, 42c, 91c, 63c

   c) 340m, 290m, 420m

   d) 1750, 1420, 2300, 1950

   e) 160g, 220g, 80g, 112g

   f) €1.99, €2.50, €1.20, €3.39

2. Here are the prices of the same basketball in a number of different shops.

   €9.95   €12.95   €10.25   €15.85

   a) Find the average price of the basketball.

   b) Which prices are above and below average?

3. Sam started reading his new book on Monday. He read 62 pages on Monday, 87 pages on Tuesday and the remaining 94 pages on Wednesday. How many pages on average did he read each day?

4. These are the scores that Gillian achieved in her last 4 maths tests: 72%, 84%, 96%, 88%.

   a) What is her average score?

   b) Which score is closest to her average score and which one is furthest from it?

5. Here are the number of newspapers a shop sold each day for a week. Find the average number of newspapers sold each day.

Monday	Tuesday	Wednesday	Thursday	Friday
316	285	229	306	384

6. Measure and record your own height and that of 4 of your friends. Find the average height of the 5 of you.

7. a) Find out the average temperature in Ireland for the month your birthday falls in. Compare it to that of the people near you.

   b) What other averages can you find out for your birthday month (hours of sunshine, amount of rainfall, etc.)? Why might this information be useful?

8. This graph shows the number of minutes Greg watched TV for a week. Examine the graph and then answer the questions.

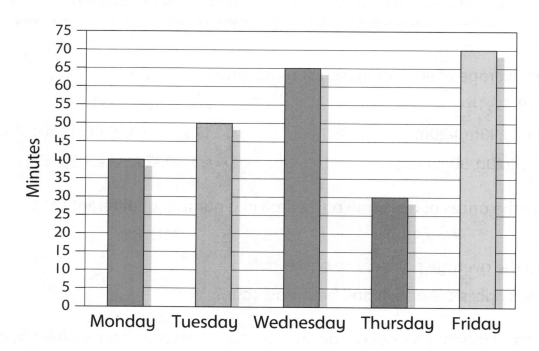

a) How many minutes in total did Greg watch TV?

b) What was the average number of minutes of TV watched per day?

c) On which days did Greg watch TV for i) an above average ii) a below average number of minutes?

d) Carry out a similar investigation yourself.

9. a) These 4 people all made the same journey of 360km. The chart shows how long the journey took each of them. Work out their average speed on the journey.

Pam	Sam	Bill	Jill
12 hours	6 hours	4 hours	2 hours

b) From your answers, can you suggest what means of transport each person was using?

More than your average puzzles?

10. The average of 3 consecutive numbers is 85. If 2 of the numbers are 85 and 86, what is the third number?

11. The average of 4 numbers is 85. The average of 3 of these numbers is 81. Find the fourth number.

12. The average of 5 square numbers is 18. If 4 of the numbers are 4, 16, 25 and 36, find the fifth number.

13. The average of 6 numbers is 22. The average of 5 of these numbers is 21. Find the sixth number.

Results of the 200m final at the Beijing Olympics

1st   Bolt, Usain, Jamaica, 19.30 seconds
2nd   Crawford, Shawn, USA, 19.96 seconds
3rd   Dix, Walter, USA, 19.98 seconds
4th   Dzingai, Brian, Zimbabwe, 20.22 seconds
5th   Malcolm, Christian, Great Britain, 20.40 seconds
6th   Collins, Kim, St Kitts/Nevis, 20.59 seconds

14. a) What was the average time for the 200m race of the 6 athletes who were awarded a time for the race? You can use a calculator.

 b) Discuss with your teacher how you might calculate the average speed of each athlete for the distance and then work it out.

 c) The fastest land animal is a cheetah. Find out the top running speed of a cheetah and see how it compares to Usain Bolt.

Homework

1. Jane has 5 uncles. Her Uncle Bob is 39. Her Uncle Bill is 47. Her Uncle Ben is 42. Her Uncle Brian is 56 and her Uncle Bert is 46. What is the average age of her 5 uncles?

2. In the last 4 seasons, No Hope City has conceded the following number of goals: 106, 98, 84 and 96. Work out the average number of goals the team has conceded over the 4 seasons.

3. The average amount of rainfall per day for December 2012 was calculated as 3mm. What was the total rainfall for the month?

4. A shop sold a total of 546 Stat Attack cards over the course of a week. What were their average daily sales?

5. The average of 5 numbers is 23. If the average of 4 of the numbers 24, what is the fifth number?

6. The following table shows the number of sweets Toothless Terry ate in one week.

Day	Monday	Tuesday	Wednesday	Thursday	Friday	Saturday	Sunday
Sweets	56	78	43	62	76	68	72

a) What was the average number of sweets Terry ate on weekdays?

b) What was the average number of sweets Terry ate at the weekend?

c) What was the average number of sweets Terry ate over the whole week?

 # Talk About

1. a) What instrument is in the picture and what do we use it to measure?
   b) What temperature does the thermometer read?
   c) Is this a warm or a cool temperature?

2. Fill in this definition:
   The freezing point of water is at ___°C and the _____ point of water is at 100°C.

3. Sort the following list into temperatures above freezing point and temperatures below freezing point.

   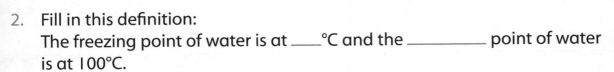

   +8°C   −5°C   −9°C   +2°C   +10°C   −3°C   0°C

4. Draw a thermometer with a scale reading from 10°C to −10°C and decide which is the warmer temperature?
   a) 4°C or 12°C   b) 6°C or 2°C   c) 1°C or −6°C   d) −2°C or −9°C

5. Which is the colder temperature? Use the thermometer you drew for questions 4 to help you.
   a) 6°C or 5° C   b) 0°C or 8°C   c) −1°C or −10°C   d) 0°C or −7°C

6. Pick 5 European capital cities and find their midday temperature today. Put the cities in order of temperature from the warmest to the coolest.

7. In a lift, what number would indicate:
   a) 2 floors above ground level
   b) 2 floors below ground level

8. A golfer scored 75 on a golf course that had a par of 72. Was the golfer's score +3, or 3 over par, or was her score −3, or 3 under par?

9. Kevin had €25 in the bank. He wrote a cheque for €30 to pay a bill. What is his bank balance now?

10. A submarine is situated in the ocean at −700 metres, or 700m below sea level. If it dives a further 200m, what is its new position?

Directed Numbers on the Number Line

These are all examples of **directed numbers**: the group of numbers that include both positive and negative numbers, or numbers above and below zero.

Have a look at these number lines showing some of the set of directed numbers.

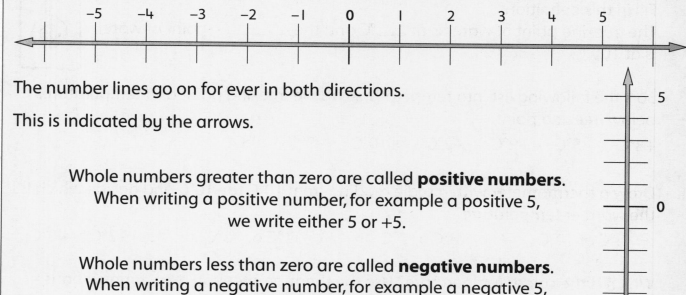

The number lines go on for ever in both directions.

This is indicated by the arrows.

Whole numbers greater than zero are called **positive numbers**.
When writing a positive number, for example a positive 5,
we write either 5 or +5.

Whole numbers less than zero are called **negative numbers**.
When writing a negative number, for example a negative 5,
we write −5.

1. Write down these numbers using the appropriate symbols (+ or −).

   a) positive 4 = + ____   b) positive 11   c) negative 2

   d) positive 15   e) negative 8   f) negative 12

   g) positive 9   h) negative 20

2. Fill in the missing numbers.

   a)
   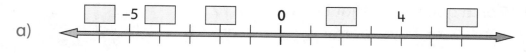

   b)
   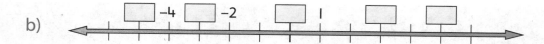

3. Draw a number line from −15 to +15 on a piece of paper (or if possible, mark it on the floor) and answer the following.

   a) How many steps does it take to get from 5 to 9?

   b) Count the number of steps from −2 to 3.

   c) How many steps does it take to get from 6 to −1?

   d) Count the number of steps from −3 to −14.

   e) Make up 5 similar questions yourself and ask the person beside you to answer them.

Puzzler

In a quiz, each team is awarded 10 points for a correct answer and 5 points are taken away for each wrong answer. If a team ended up with a score of −15 points and we know that they got 6 answers right, how many wrong answers did these geniuses give?

4. Use your number line to find which is greater. (Hint: as you move to the left (or down) on the number line, numbers get smaller in value.)

   a) 6 or 3   b) 7 or 14   c) 2 or −2   d) 0 or −5

   e) −5 or 1   f) −1 or −10   g) −5 or −2   h) 1 or 0

5. Using your number line, write 3 whole numbers that are:

   a) Greater than zero

   b) Less than zero

   c) Greater than −7 but less than −2

   d) Greater than negative 6 but less than positive 4

   e) Less than positive 5 but greater than negative 1

   f) Greater than −9 but less than +9

Ordering and Sequencing Directed Numbers

1. Continue these sequences of directed numbers.

   a) 3, 2, 1, ____, ____, ____, ____, ____, ____

   b) −15, −13, −11, −9, ____, ____, ____, ____, ____

   c) 20, 15, 10, 5, ____, ____, ____, ____, ____

   d) −3, −6, −9, −12, ____, ____, ____, ____, ____

   e) 40, 30, 20, ____, ____, ____, ____, ____, ____

   f) −8, −4, 0, 4, ____, ____, ____, ____, ____

   g) 150, 100, 50, ____, ____, ____, ____, ____, ____

2. Use positive or negative numbers to represent the following.

   a) 32 degrees Celsius above zero

   b) diving at 15m below sea level

   c) A bank account being overdrawn by €25

   d) One floor below ground level on a lift

   e) Climbing a mountain at 850m above sea level

3. Put the numbers in these lists in order, starting with the number of greatest value.

   a) +1, −4, +12, +8, −6, −15, +9, +3, +20, −3

   b) −9, +25, 0, −5, +5, +8, −20, +1, +6, +10, −10

   c) +2, −7, +3, −2, +18, +11, −19, +8, −11, −1, 0

   d) 0, −30, +29, −50, −45, +55, +21, −32, +37, −25, +60

   e) In the above questions, why does 0 have neither a positive (+) nor a negative (−) sign?

Adding Positive and Negative Numbers

1. The tide comes in and out each morning and evening around the coast of Ireland. If the tide is due to come in at 4:40am in Kinsale, work out the time it will come in at in each of these towns from the information given.

   Bantry: +12 minutes   Castletownbere: −3 minutes

   Dingle: −8 minutes   Schull: +15 minutes

   Tralee: +5 minutes   Cahirciveen: −33 minutes

The temperature at dawn in Moscow was −3°C. By midday the temperature had risen by +7°C. What was the temperature at midday?

Our sum looks like this: −3 + +7 = _____.

To work out our answer, use the number line.

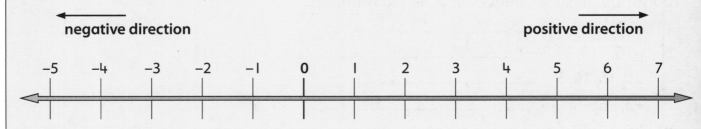

We start at −3. We are **adding** on +7, so we face the **positive direction**.

Since it's a +7, we **count on** 7. We land at +4, so −3 + +7 = +4.

Temperature = +4°C

At dusk, the temperature in Moscow dropped to −1°C.
As night fell, the temperature dropped a further 5°C.
What temperature was it that night?

Our sum looks like this: −1 + −5 = _____.

Use your number line. We start at −1. We are **adding** on −5,
so we face the **negative direction**.

Since we are adding −5, we must **count back** 5. We land at −6, so −1 + −5 = −6.

Temperature = −6°C

2. Now have a go at these. Remember to use your number line to help you.

a) +5 + −2   b) +7 + +4   c) +8 + −5
d) −2 + +7   e) −1 + −6   f) +10 + −12
g) +4 + −8   h) −8 + +2   i) −2 + −9

3. Here is a chart of today's weather forecast in some American cities. The temperature
for the morning is given and the predicted rise or fall in temperature for the day.
Can you work out the afternoon temperature for each city?

City	Morning temperature	Rise/fall in °C	Afternoon temperature
Boston	+4°C	Fall: −5°C	
Chicago	−3°C	Rise: +8°C	
New York	+8°C	Fall: −7°C	
Miami	−1°C	Rise: +6°C	
Dallas	+10°C	Fall: −13°C	

Banks use the system of credit and debit according to
whether you are putting money into or taking money out
of your account.

To be allowed to go below zero in your bank account,
you need to set up an overdraft. If you had an overdraft
of €100, you could be overdrawn on your account up to
−€100 and owe it to the bank.

4. This is a bank statement of an account that has an overdraft of €50. Can you fill in any missing amounts before it's sent to the customer?

Date	Details	Debit €	Credit €	Balance €
1 Jan	Balance			20.00
6 Jan	Withdrawal	10.00		
8 Jan	Withdrawal	15.00		
12 Jan	Deposit		20.00	
17 Jan	Withdrawal	5.00		
21 Jan	Withdrawal	30.00		
22 Jan	Deposit		15.00	
25 Jan	Deposit		10.00	
27 Jan	Withdrawal	5.00		
1 Feb	Deposit		20.00	

5. Invent your own bank statement with an overdraft of €100. Fill in the debits and credits and let the person beside you work out the balance.

6. Mrs Rich had €55 in the bank. She spent €65 with her Laser card. What is her bank balance now?

7. Mr Penniless had a bank balance of –€15.00, but luckily he won the weekly prize draw of €35.00. How much money does he have in his account now?

8. A bank customer has a balance of –€20 and makes a payment of €50 into the account. How much money is in the account now?

9. A diver is diving at –15m (15m below sea level) and rises by 8m. What depth is the diver at now?

10. A plane is flying at an altitude of 8000m and rises a further 22000m before levelling off. What altitude is the plane flying at now?

11. Nicola gets onto a lift at 2 floors below ground level, or level –2. She wants to go up 5 floors to the shopping area. On what level is the shopping area?

12. Golf uses directed numbers in its scoring. This table shows the scores of the first round of the golf championships. Using the information given, work out how much over or under par each of the players was.

Name	Score 1st round
Ryan	71
Byrne	67
Fleming	73
Flanagan	70
O'Connor	66

The number of golf strokes (or par) the golfers should have taken for this course was 69.

So if a golfer scored 72, they would have a score of +3, or 3 over par.

If a golfer scored 65, they would have a score of – 4, or 4 under par.

The winner is the golfer who is the most under par, or takes the fewest number of strokes to complete the course.

13. Here are the results of each player over the next 3 rounds. Work out how much over or under par each of the players was in each round and then work out their final score relative to par.

Ryan: 70, 67, 66   **Byrne:** 66, 68, 72
Fleming: 70, 67, 70   **Flanagan:** 65, 71, 67
O'Connor: 66, 70, 65

Homework

1. Penny Less had €24.36 left in her bank account, but her bank allows her to be overdrawn up to €50 and she wants to buy a pair of shoes. Work out how much she would be overdrawn for each pair of shoes she might buy.

a) €47.99   b) €35.85   c) €56.29

d) €63.78  e) €92.42  f) €71.57

2. Which pair of shoes would the bank have a problem with Penny buying? Why?

3. The following are the scores of some golfers in the first and second rounds of a golf tournament. The par of the course is 68.

Player	1st round score	2nd round score
Harry Hacker	77	68
Sally Slice	59	79
Wally Driver	71	73
Sharon Shanks	85	62
Sandy Lie	64	71
Panther Forest	67	74

a) Can you work out how far above or below par each player was in the first round?

b) Can you work out how far above or below par each player was in the second round?

c) When you put the 2 scores together, how far above or below par is each player?

d) If only 2 rounds were played in the tournament, who was the winner?

Recap

· I can identify directed numbers on a number line. ○ ○ ○

· I can order directed numbers. ○ ○ ○

· I can add directed numbers. ○ ○ ○

· I can add directed numbers in different contexts. ○ ○ ○

 Talk About

1. Can you identify these instruments used for weighing objects? Give an example of 2 items you would weigh using each of these instruments.

a)    b)    c)    d)

2. Name 5 items around your classroom that you think weigh
   a) less than 100g   b) more than 100g. Check your answers.

3. Find out which of the following items is the lightest. Estimate the weight of each, select the appropriate unit and weigh them using the appropriate instrument.
   a) a chair   b) 5 encyclopaedias
   c) a printer   d) a schoolbag

Item	Unit	Estimated weight	Actual weight	Difference

   e) Select 5 more items from your schoolbag and find which is the heaviest using the same chart.

4. Estimate which item is heavier.
   a) A cushion or a calculator
   b) A wooden block or cement brick of the same size
   c) A golf ball or a balloon
   d) A kilogram of lead or a kilogram of air

Grams and Kilograms

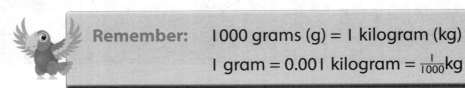

Remember: 1000 grams (g) = 1 kilogram (kg)

1 gram = 0.001 kilogram = $\frac{1}{1000}$kg

1. Choose the correct weight.
    a) Does a jar of jam weigh 450 grams or 450 kilograms?
    b) Does a small boat weigh 2500 grams or 2500 kilograms?
    c) Does a laptop computer weigh 10 grams or 10 kilograms?
    d) Does a cup weigh 40 grams or 40 kilograms?

Remember: there are a number of different ways to write the same weight. For example:
6350g = 6kg 350g

2. Fill in the gaps.
    a) 2670g = ____kg _____g
    b) 1265g = ____kg _____g
    c) 9062g = ____kg _____g
    d) 4kg 932g = _____g
    e) 6kg 9g = _____g
    f) 8kg 20g = _____g
    g) 6050g = ____kg _____g
    h) 3kg 754g = _____g
    i) 4030g = ____kg _____g

> Weights can also be written as fractions or decimals of a kilogram. For example:
> 1kg 500g = 1500g = 1.5kg

3. Complete the table.

2kg 250g	2250g	2.25kg
	1378g	
		3.86kg
28kg 375g		
	19006g	
		7.1kg
12kg 005g		
	82079g	

> We can also record measurements of weight as fractions or decimals. For example:
> 1kg 465g = $1\frac{465}{1000}$kg = 1.465kg

4. Now complete this table.

Measurement	Fraction	Decimal
1593g		
		7.15kg
	$8\frac{158}{1000}$kg	
346g		
	$2\frac{3}{4}$kg	
		3.7kg
6008g		
	$4\frac{17}{1000}$kg	
		9.045kg

5. a) How much lighter than 6.7kg is 5700g?

   b) How much lighter than 15kg 460g is 15.3kg?

   c) How many grams must be added to 4kg 210g to make 4.3kg?

   d) How many grams must be added to 6.9kg to make 7200g?

   e) How much heavier than 11.1kg is 11kg 345g?

   f) How much heavier than 24kg 590g is 24.65kg?

Adding and Subtracting Weights

A butcher cut up a large piece of beef into 3 smaller pieces to be sold. They weighed 1890g, 2kg 35g and 3.8kg. What was the total weight of the large piece of meat?

When adding weights, each weight must be written using the same units. Here are the 3 possibilities:

g	kg	g	kg
1890	1	890	1.890
2035	2	035	2.035
+ 3800	+ 3	800	+ 3.800

Check to see that the answers are the same.

6. Now try these. Remember to change them to the same units before you start.

    a)   3760g + 2kg 907g + 11.5kg   b)   12.65kg + 9003g + 10kg 980g

    c)   16.84kg + 21kg 530g + 5392g   d)   18.8kg + 12930g + 8kg 7g

    e)   739g + 2kg 83g + 36.2kg   f)   20kg 5g + 19.02kg + 18g

7. William's schoolbag weighs 6kg 8g and Deirdre's weighs 4.02kg. How much heavier is William's schoolbag?

8. Now try these. Remember to change measurements to the same unit first.

    a) 6950g – 3.01kg   b) 14kg 12g – 8669g   c) 21.5kg – 370g

    d) 16700g – 10kg 7g   e) 55kg 758g – 44.8kg   f) 179.2kg – 97kg 2g

Kilograms and Tonnes

Remember: 1000 kilograms (kg) = 1 tonne (t)

Minnie – 845.8kg

Hefty – 998kg 35g

Bulky – 805kg 9g

1. a)   Which whale is the heaviest?

    b)   What weight are Minnie and Bulky added together?

    c)   What weight are Hefty and Teeny added together?

    d)   Which 2 whales added together would be the heaviest?

Teeny – 902.487kg

    e)   If all 4 whales were on very big weighing scales, what would their combined weight be?

    f)   How much heavier is the heaviest whale than the lightest whale?

2. A large container ship has 3 crates weighing 780.6kg, 640kg 320g and 810.07kg. How much less than 2500kg (or 2.5 tonnes) is their combined weight?

A lion and a tiger stood on a weighing scales together, which showed their combined weight as 126kg. When the lion stood on the scales with a fox, their combined weight was 82kg. When the tiger stood on the scales with the fox, their combined weight was 74kg. Work out the individual weights of the lion, the tiger and the fox.

Multiplying and Dividing Weights

A box of cornflakes weighs 1kg 125g. How much would a crate of 65 such boxes weigh?

We can write this question in 3 different ways.

g	kg	g	kg
1125	1	125	1.125
× 65	×	65	× 65

1. Now have a go at these.

    a) 6.865kg × 5

    b) 8kg 287g × 6

    c) 12.9kg × 18

    d) 8492g × 94

    e) 9.25kg × 48

    f) 9481g × 16

    g) 176kg 20g × 60

    h) 19.8kg × 99

    i) 8301g × 22

2. A tin of peas weighs 345g. How heavy would 92 of these tins be?

3. A small car weighs 9540kg. A transporter weighing 25 tonnes (25000kg) was carrying 12 of these small cars. Find the total weight of the cars and transporter.

228.88kg of logs were divided into 8 bags to be sold. What was the weight of the logs in each bag?

8 | 228.88kg

4. Try these division questions. Remember to give the units for each answer.

    a) 32.85kg ÷ 9

    b) 312kg 400g ÷ 5

    c) 177kg 884g ÷ 7

    d) 5kg 400g ÷ 15

    e) 996.6kg ÷ 22

    f) 7kg 471g ÷ 31

    g) 40.152kg ÷ 42

    h) 7kg 80g ÷ 59

    i) 18kg 957g ÷ 89

5. Try these using your calculator.

    a) (459.82kg + 830kg 2g) − 500.748kg

    b) (1.734kg + 3kg 832g) ÷ 46

    c) (76.94kg × 56) − 947kg 3g

    d) 673.549kg − (12.274kg × 18)

Homework

1. Can you write these as kilograms and grams?

   a) 1006g

   b) 2674g

   c) 9603g

   d) 2.6kg

   e) 1.768kg

   f) 7.08kg

   g) 290g

   h) 5.1kg

   i) 8.036kg

2. Fill in the gaps.

g	kg g	kg
	2kg 508g	
693g		
		7.268g
	9kg 4g	
		6.01kg

3. Now try these. Remember to change them to the same units before you start.

   a) 4352g + 1kg 746g + 3.809kg

   b) 2.07kg + 6080g + 1kg 247g

   c) 3.27kg + 2kg 93g + 725g

   d) 5kg 184g + 2.504kg + 7176g

   e) 3.465kg + 8kg 2g + 5231g

   f) 4kg 180g + 0.739kg + 9014g

4. Now try these subtraction questions, again changing weights to the same unit first.

   a) 5kg 157g – 2.96kg

   b) 8013g – 4kg 75g

   c) 8.243kg – 5739g

   d) 9kg 254g – 6.837kg

   e) 7682g – 3.486kg

   f) 8kg 17g – 695g

5. Now try these.

   a) 647g × 9

   b) 3kg 185g × 7

   c) 5.28kg × 8

   d) 4kg 59g × 18

   e) 7196g × 24

   f) 3.059kg × 37

6. Now try these.

   a) 5.184kg ÷ 8

   b) 6kg 444g ÷ 9

   c) 1716g ÷ 6

   d) 26.86kg ÷ 17

   e) 8kg 586g ÷ 27

   f) 89.42kg ÷ 34

7. What is the total weight of 39 books if each book weighs 1.487 kilograms?

8. Brian had 3 bags of shopping when he came back from the supermarket. The first weighed 5kg 362g, the second weighed 3097g and the third weighed 6.03kg. What was the total weight of the 3 bags?

9. Sandra's schoolbag weighs 9.68kg. If the books she takes out for her homework weigh a total of 2kg 38g, how much does her schoolbag now weigh?

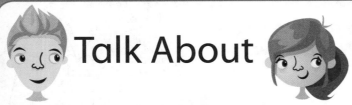 ## Talk About

Puzzler

Look at this trend graph carefully. Use your powers of deduction to work out what it might represent.

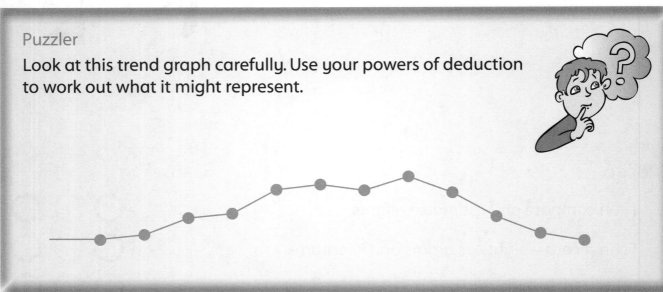

A **pie chart** is a way of representing data. It's easy to compare results when they are drawn as sections of a circle.

Collect as many examples of pie charts from newspapers or magazines as you can find. Describe the information being shown in each pie chart.

2.7% 10.1%

20.5%

15.5%

36.1%

15.1%

- Sinn Féin
- Independent
- Fianna Fáil
- Fine Gael
- Labour
- Other

Examine the pie chart above and describe the information being given.

Reading and Interpreting Pie Charts

1. 48 children were surveyed on their method of transport to school. The pie chart shows the results.

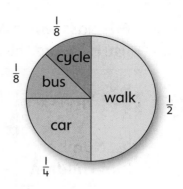

   a) Which is the most popular method of transport?

   b) Can you figure out how many children use each method of transport?

   (For example: $\frac{1}{2}$ walk to school and $\frac{1}{2}$ of 48 = _____.)

   Remember: 1 full rotation = 360°.

   c) Find how many degrees are in each section of the pie chart.

   walk to school = $\frac{1}{2}$ of full rotation = $\frac{1}{2}$ of 360° = _____°

   by car = $\frac{1}{4}$ of full rotation = $\frac{1}{4}$ of 360° = _____°

   by bicycle or by bus = $\frac{1}{8}$ of full rotation = $\frac{1}{8}$ of 360° = _____°

2. Now find these.

   a) $\frac{1}{5}$ of 360°   b) $\frac{3}{4}$ of 360°   c) $\frac{1}{10}$ of 360°   d) $\frac{5}{6}$ of 360°

3. The following pie chart shows last year's summer holiday destinations of a group of people. Examine the chart and then answer the questions that follow.

   a) How many people were surveyed altogether?

   b) What was the most popular holiday destination last year of those surveyed?

   c) What was the least popular holiday destination last year of those surveyed?

   d) What percentage of the people travelled to Spain?

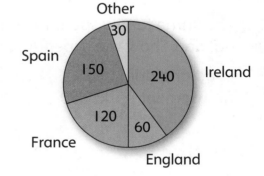

   e) Calculate the angle of each section of the pie chart.

   For example: Ireland = $\frac{240}{600}$ = $\frac{2}{5}$ and $\frac{2}{5}$ of 360° = _____°

   England = $\frac{60}{600}$ = $\frac{1}{10}$ and $\frac{1}{10}$ of 360° = _____°

4. A prize of €200 for an art competition was shared among 4 people. From the pie chart, can you work out how much money each person received?

   Sinead: 40% of €200 = €_____

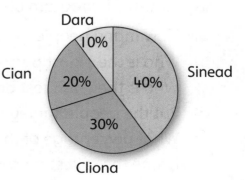

Constructing a Pie Chart

1. a) 6th class was asked to choose their favourite sport from the following list. Here are the results. Display these results on a pie chart.

Sport	Gaelic	Hurling/ camogie	Soccer	Basketball	Hockey
Number of children	10	5	15	15	5

> To find out how many degrees are in each section of the pie chart, we must find what fraction of the total number of children like each sport.
>
> $$Total = 10 + 5 + 15 + 15 + 5 = 50$$
>
> $$Gaelic: \frac{10}{50} = \frac{1}{5}$$
>
> To find the size of the angle that will represent this on the pie chart, we find $\frac{1}{5}$ of $360° = $ _____.
>
> When all of the angles have been calculated, draw a full circle and divide it up accordingly using your protractor.
>
> Remember to label each fraction of your pie chart.

b) Carry out a similar investigation in your own class.

2. The Byrne family spent the following amounts on their holiday. Show their spending on a pie chart.

Food and drink: €250   Car hire: €100
Amusement park: €50   Water sports: €100

Compiling and Interpreting Data Sets

3. Collect a complete set of data on your classmates. What information will you require? Remember to include data such as height, age, shoe size, hair colour, etc. Add in a few unusual questions! How will you record your information? If possible, record the data in a database program on a computer.

a) How many people in total have contributed to your data set?

b) Who is the oldest person recorded?

c) Who is the youngest person recorded?

d) Put the people surveyed in order, from youngest to oldest.

e) What percentage of the people surveyed have brown hair?

f) Name the tallest person surveyed.

g) Name the smallest person surveyed.

h) What is the average height of the people surveyed?

i) What fraction of the names of the people surveyed begin with a vowel?

j) Make up 5 more questions based on your set of data.

k) Draw a pie chart to display the shoe size of the people surveyed.

Choose 3 pieces of data from your set, e.g. eye colour, and display your results on an appropriate graph.

4. Carry out a class survey on food eaten. Classify food into various categories, e.g. fruit, vegetables, and display the data on as many graphs as possible. From the graphs, pick the most / least popular food in each category.

5. Pick I of the following topics to carry out a survey on. Collect, organise and display your data set in an appropriate way.

a) Cereals eaten for breakfast

b) Favourite pop group

c) Number of hours of sunshine each day for a week.

d) Number of seconds taken to say the alphabet backwards

Homework

1. Find:

a) $\frac{1}{4}$ of 360°   b) $\frac{1}{6}$ of 360°   c) $\frac{1}{8}$ of 360°   d) $\frac{3}{8}$ of 360°

2. This pie chart shows what the preferred birthday present would be for 140 children. From the pie chart, work out how many children preferred each present.

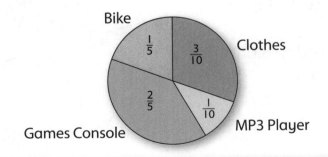

 # Talk About

1. True or false?
   a) Area is a measure of the amount of space contained inside a 2-D shape.
   b) You can measure space with a ruler.
   c) You can work out the area of a rectangle if you know its length and its width.
   d) A square metre is bigger than a square centimetre.
   e) There are 100 square centimetres in a square metre.
   f) 2 rectangles with different lengths and widths can have the same area.
   g) The area of a rectangle is calculated by adding the length and the width.

2. If you were about to do the following activities, what would be more important: area or perimeter?
   a) Buying carpet for a floor
   b) Buying wire to build a fence around your garden
   c) Ordering paving stones to build a path around your house
   d) Buying enough paint to cover the back wall of your garden
   e) Buying grass seed to plant in a new garden

Calculating Area

3. If you were to write a rule about how to work out the area of a rectangle, how would you write it? Try it first with words and when you have done that, change it to symbols.

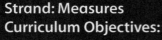

Strand: Measures
Curriculum Objectives:
Recognise that the length of the perimeter of a rectangular shape does not determine the area of the shape;
calculate the area of regular and irregular 2-D shapes;

4. Now work out the area of these rectangles. Remember to record the correct unit of measurement in your answer (cm² or m²).

Rectangle 1
Length – 26cm
Width – 18cm
Area – ?

Rectangle 2
Length – 13cm
Width – 6.9cm
Area – ?

Rectangle 3
Length – 5.7m
Width – 4.8m
Area – ?

Rectangle 4
Length – 15.3m
Width – 7.5m
Area – ?

Rectangle 5
Length – 10.7cm
Width – 9.1cm
Area – ?

Rectangle 6
Length – 14m
Width – 9.56m
Area – ?

5. A principal bought new lino to put on the floors of 4 of the classrooms in the school.

   a) If each of the classrooms was 9.7m × 13m, how much lino did she need?

   b) What was the total cost if the lino cost €19 per square metre?

6. Before putting down the lino, the principal had the noticeboards painted. If each of the 4 noticeboards was 2.8m long and 1.5m wide and a tin of paint would cover 5.6 square metres of noticeboard, how many tins of paint did the principal need to buy?

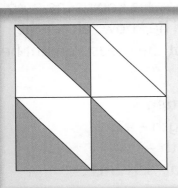

Puzzler
This square is 8cm in length.
What is the area of the shaded section?

area = length × width
132 = ? × 11
So length = 12cm

?cm

11cm

Area = 132cm²

Make the rule by filling in the blanks in this sentence.

If you know the area of a rectangle and you also know either the length or the width, you can work out the side you don't know by _____ the _____ by the _____.

7. A gardener has to cut the grass in each of the following gardens. He knows the area of each of the gardens because he planted the grass seed and he knows either the length or the width of each garden. Can you help him work out the measurement he is missing?

Garden 1
Length – ?
Width – 16m
Area – 304m²

Garden 2
Length – 38m
Width – ?
Area – 912m²

Garden 3
Length – 42m
Width – ?
Area – 1512m²

Garden 4
Length – ?
Width – 15m
Area – 705m²

Garden 5
Length – ?
Width – 27m
Area – 729m²

Garden 6
Length – ?
Width – 30m
Area – 1620m²

8. If the area of a garden is 238m² and the length of the garden is 17m, what is the width of the garden?

9. a) If the perimeter of a piece of paper is 112cm and the width of the piece of paper is 27cm, what is the area of the piece of paper?

    b) If I have a second piece of paper whose perimeter is 114cm and whose length is 39cm, what is the area of the piece of paper?

    c) Compare the perimeters and areas of the 2 pieces of paper. What do you notice about your answers?

Area and Perimeter

1. Look at these 2 rectangles that have exactly the same perimeter.

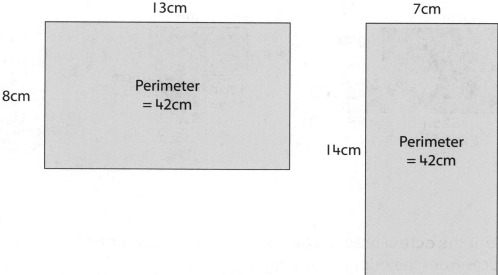

13cm

7cm

8cm

Perimeter
= 42cm

14cm

Perimeter
= 42cm

a) Will their areas be exactly the same?

b) If not, which of the 2 rectangles will have the greater area?

c) Now work out the areas of both rectangles and see if you were right.

2. Now try these. In each case, first guess which of the rectangles has the greater area and then check to see if you are right.

Rectangle A
Perimeter – 158cm
Length – 48cm
Width – ?
Area – ?

Rectangle B
Perimeter – 158cm
Length – ?
Width – 27cm
Area – ?

Rectangle C
Perimeter – 206cm
Length – ?
Width – 39cm
Area – ?

Rectangle D
Perimeter – 206cm
Length – ?
Width – 48cm
Area – ?

Rectangle E
Perimeter – 232cm
Length – 58cm
Width – ?
Area – ?

Rectangle F
Perimeter – 232cm
Length – ?
Width – 43cm
Area – ?

What conclusion can you draw from your answers? Is there any pattern? Discuss this with the people near you and then try to complete this sentence.

If 2 rectangles have the same perimeter, the rectangle with the greater area will be the rectangle whose dimensions are _____.

Calculating the Area of Irregular Shapes

1. What would the areas of these rectangles be if pieces hadn't been removed?

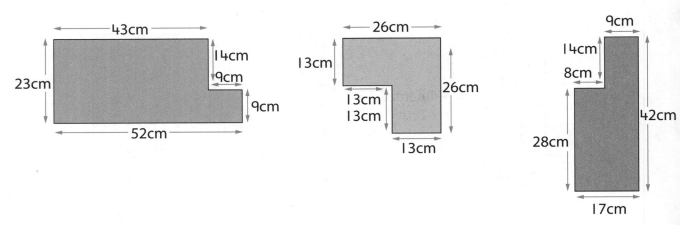

2. Now work out the actual area of each of the shapes by subtracting the area of the missing pieces from the original rectangles.

Surface Area

How many faces does a cube have? What shape is each of the faces?

We can measure the area of a face of the cube. Each of the faces of the cube will have exactly the same area.

When we put the areas of all of the faces of the cube together, we get the total **surface area** of the cube.

Look at a cube with an edge of 5cm.   5cm

When we open it out into its net, it's easier for us to see.

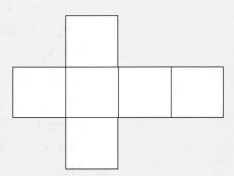

Each of the 6 faces will have exactly the same area – 5cm × 5cm – so the surface area of the cube will be the combined area of all 6 faces.

$$5cm \times 5cm = 25cm^2 \times 6 = 150cm^2 = surface\ area$$

1. Conor is sending a parcel in the post that is cube shaped. He wants to make sure that it doesn't get soggy if it starts raining, so he decides to cover the parcel in contact paper but he doesn't know how much he will need. He needs to work out the surface area of the parcel because he will need enough contact paper to cover its surface area (and a little bit extra, of course!). If an edge of the parcel is measured at 9cm, what is the surface area of the parcel?

9cm

2. Now work out the surface areas of these cube-shaped parcels.

Parcel 1
Edge – 7cm

Parcel 2
Edge – 12cm

Parcel 3
Edge – 14cm

Parcel 4
Edge – 23cm

Parcel 5
Edge – 29cm

Parcel 6
Edge – 35cm

We can also measure the total surface area of a cuboid.

How many faces does a cuboid have? What shapes are the faces of the cuboid?

If we open up the cuboid into a net, we can see the different shapes very clearly.

The cuboid is made up of 4 rectangles and 2 squares.

How many measurements do we need to know to work out the surface area of the cuboid?

If 1 of the rectangles is 7cm long and 5cm wide, what is the total surface area of the cuboid?

7cm × 5cm = 35cm^2 × 4 = 140cm^2
5cm × 5cm = 25cm^2 × 2 = 50cm^2 140cm^2 + 50cm^2 = 190cm^2

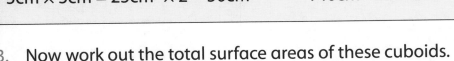

3. Now work out the total surface areas of these cuboids.

Cuboid 1
Length – 9cm
Width – 4cm
Surface area – ?

Cuboid 2
Length – 8cm
Width – 6cm
Surface area – ?

Cuboid 3
Length – 12cm
Width – 11cm
Surface area – ?

Cuboid 4
Length – 14cm
Width – 7cm
Surface area – ?

Cuboid 5
Length – 19cm
Width – 13cm
Surface area – ?

Cuboid 6
Length – 25cm
Width – 17cm
Surface area – ?

4. a) Joe got a surprise present for his birthday. It came in a cuboid-shaped box that was 16cm long and 11cm wide. What was the total surface area of the present?

    b) In his excitement to see what was inside the box, Joe ripped the 2 square ends off the box. What was the total surface area of the box then?

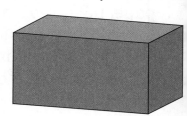

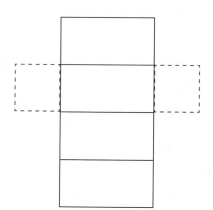

The nets of some cuboids look like this.

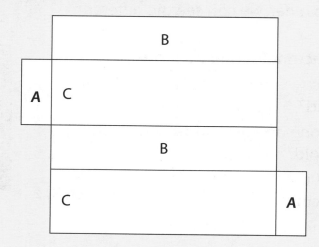

This net is made up of 3 different rectangles.

To work out the total surface area in this situation, we need a third dimension, but which measurement is it? What do we call this dimension?

If this cuboid is 10cm long, 5cm wide and the third dimension is 2cm, how do we work out the total surface area?

Rectangle A = 2cm × 5cm = 10cm²
Rectangle B = 10cm × 2cm = 20cm²
Rectangle C = 10cm × 5cm = 50cm²

Now calculate the total surface area.

5. Calculate the total surface areas of cuboids with the following 3 dimensions.

Cuboid	1st dimension	2nd dimension	3rd dimension	Surface area
A	6cm	4cm	3cm	
B	9cm	7cm	5cm	
C	12cm	8cm	2cm	
D	15cm	5cm	6cm	
E	11cm	18cm	8cm	
F	22cm	14cm	4cm	

Homework

1. Work out the area of these rectangles. Remember to record the correct unit of
    measurement in your answer (cm² or m²).

Rectangle 1
Length – 23cm
Width – 17cm
Area – ?

Rectangle 2
Length – 37cm
Width – 26cm
Area – ?

Rectangle 3
Length – 9.3m
Width – 2.5m
Area – ?

Rectangle 4
Length – 13.8m
Width – 6.4m
Area – ?

Rectangle 5
Length – 12.9cm
Width – 8.6cm
Area – ?

Rectangle 6
Length – 19m
Width – 7.38m
Area – ?

2. Now find the missing dimension of each of these fields.

Field 1
Length – ?
Width – 17m
Area – 391m²

Field 2
Length – ?
Width – 26m
Area – 884m²

Field 3
Length – 39m
Width – ?
Area – 702m²

Field 4
Length – 35m
Width – ?
Area – 980m²

Field 5
Length – ?
Width – 18m
Area – 828m²

Field 6
Length – 48m
Width – ?
Area – 1344m²

3. In the following table, posters 1 and 2 have the same perimeter, posters 3 and 4 have the same perimeter and posters 5 and 6 have the same perimeter. See how their areas compare by working out the missing dimensions and then calculating their area.

Poster	Perimeter	Area	Length	Width
1	156cm		43cm	
2	156cm			29cm
3	244cm			56cm
4	244cm		74cm	
5	272cm		62cm	
6	272cm			86cm

4. Work out the area and perimeter of these unusual shapes.

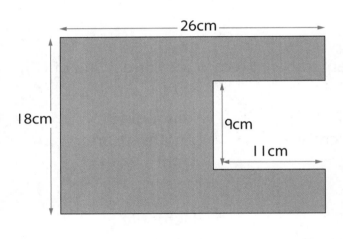

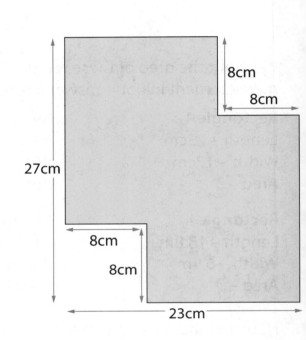

5. Work out the surface areas of these cubes.

Cube 1
Edge – 9cm

Cube 2
Edge – 11cm

Cube 3
Edge – 15cm

Cube 4
Edge – 18cm

Cube 5
Edge – 26cm

Cube 6
Edge – 34cm

5. Now work out the total surface areas of these cuboids.

Cuboid 1
Length – 7cm
Width – 5cm
Surface area – ?

Cuboid 2
Length – 9cm
Width – 4cm
Surface area – ?

Cuboid 3
Length – 12cm
Width – 8cm
Surface area – ?

Cuboid 4
Length – 16cm
Width – 7cm
Surface area – ?

Cuboid 5
Length – 18cm
Width – 14cm
Surface area – ?

Cuboid 6
Length – 27cm
Width – 19cm
Surface area – ?

Recap

- I can work out missing measurements.   ○ ○ ○

- I can work out the area of an irregular shape.   ○ ○ ○

- I know what surface area is.   ○ ○ ○

- I can work out the surface area of a cube.   ○ ○ ○

- I can work out the surface area of a cuboid.   ○ ○ ○

 Talk About

1. Find 5 containers that hold liquid and place them in order, starting with the container that holds the most to the container that holds the least.

2. Name 5 liquids that you would find in your classroom.

3. Find 5 different types of bottle. Place them in order, starting with the one that you think holds the most to the one that holds the least. Fill the bottle that you think holds the most with water. Pour this water into the next bottle until it's full. Pour the water from the second bottle into the third bottle and so on until you have filled the fifth bottle. If you have guessed the order of the bottles correctly, what should be left in each bottle?

Remember: Capacity is a measure of the amount of liquid a container can hold.

4. List these containers in order of capacity.

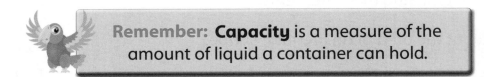

Millilitres and Litres

What unit is used to measure capacity: **grams**, **litres** or **metres**?

$$1000 \text{ millilitres (ml)} = 1 \text{ litre}$$

$$1 \text{ ml} = \tfrac{1}{1000}l = 0.001 \, l$$

1. Draw and label 6 liquids you can buy in containers that are measured in
   a) litres
   b) millilitres.

2. Choose the correct capacity.
   a) Does a carton of milk have a capacity of 1 millilitre or 1 litre?
   b) Does a teaspoon have a capacity of 5 millilitres or 5 litres?
   c) Does a car's petrol tank have a capacity of 40 millilitres or 40 litres?
   d) Does a fish tank have a capacity of 10 millilitres or 10 litres?
   e) Does an egg cup hold 25 millilitres or 25 litres?

3. We use a graduated jug to measure the exact capacity of containers. How much liquid is in each graduated jug?

Remember: 1 litre = 1000 millilitres

4. How many millilitres?
   a) If there is $\frac{1}{4}$l of milk left in a carton, how many millilitres of milk are left?
   b) If I poured $\frac{1}{2}$l of juice into a jug, how many millilitres of juice are in the jug?
   c) A bottle has a capacity of $\frac{3}{4}$l. How many millilitres does it hold?

5. Can you write these as litres and millilitres?
   a) 1129ml
   b) 6042ml
   c) 2105ml
   d) 1009ml
   e) 5228ml
   f) 3785ml
   g) 7960ml
   h) 1.5l
   i) 9.6l

6. Put these containers in order, starting with the container that holds the least amount of liquid.

Capacities can be recorded in a number of different ways. For example:
2375ml = 2l 375ml = 2.375l

7. Fill in the blanks.

ml	l ml	l
4200ml		
	2l 500ml	
		6.482l
9820ml		

We can also record measurements of capacity as fractions or decimals.
1l 465ml = $1\frac{465}{1000}$l = 1.465l

8. Now fill in the blanks in this table.

Measurement	Fraction	Decimal
2987ml		
		4.35l
	$5\frac{239}{1000}$l	
7001ml		
	$5\frac{1}{4}$l	
		8.9l
692ml		
	$1\frac{23}{1000}$l	
		5.027l

9. How would you compare the cost of champagne and lemonade?

10. Find the price of a 1l container of milk and the price of a 2l container of milk. Is it cheaper to buy the 2l container?

11. a) Find an empty 330ml can and a 2l bottle. How many cans can be filled from the bottle?

    b) Find a drink that is sold in these 2 containers and compare the cost.

Puzzler

You have a 5l bottle and a 7l bottle that you can fill and empty as often as you like. You can pour from one bottle to another, refill and pour away as much as you need to. The bottles do not have a regular shape. How can you measure 1l of water?

Volume

- The word *capacity* can mean a lot of different things, but in this context it refers to the amount of liquid an object or container can hold.
- The unit of measurement is the litre, or l.
- The volume of an object is not how loud it is but the amount of space that the object occupies.
- The unit we use to measure volume is called the cubic centimetre, or cm³.

What do you think a cubic centimetre looks like?
(The hint is in the name.)

Draw one in your copy and then compare it to the one of the person beside you.

Why might this be a good unit for measuring volume?
What about a spherical centimetre?

1. Collect either a 1 litre cardboard carton of milk or a 1 litre tub of ice cream. Wash out the container and carefully remove 1 side. (Hint: This is much easier if the container already has a removable lid!) Using 1cm cubes, fill the container, leaving no empty spaces.

   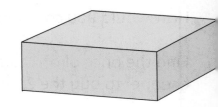

   Record the number of cubes you use = _____cm³

2. Find 3 other cuboid boxes and carry out the same experiment. Record the number of 1cm cubes you need to fill the box in each case.

   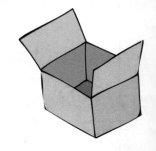

   Volume of the box = number of cubes used = _____cm³

3. a) Fill a litre cuboid container completely with water. How many litres of water does it hold?

   b) Dry out the container and now fill it with 1cm cubes, leaving no spaces. How many cubes does it take to fill the container? _____cm³

   c) So what do you think the relationship is between litres and cubic centimetres?

Adding and Subtracting Capacity

For her party, Adele has bought 6 litres of orange. She fills 3 jugs, which have a capacity of 1.25l, 2l 430ml and 2035ml. How much orange will she have left over after she has filled each of the jugs?

We must first add the capacities of the jugs. There are a few ways of adding capacities. See if you get the same answer for each.

a) ml	b) litres millilitres	c) litres
1250	1 250	1.250
2430	2 430	2.430
+ 2035	+ 2 035	+ 2.035

When we have this answer, we must then subtract our answer from 6 litres to find how much extra orange Adele has.

4. Now try these. Remember to change them to the same units before you start.

   a) 7652ml + 11 594ml + 2.8l

   b) 2.675l + 128ml + 2l 739ml

   c) 1.7l + 9l 32ml + 2096ml

   d) 4.287l + 2007ml + 2l 9ml

   e) 967ml + 2l 674ml + 8.2l

   f) 1l 85ml + 5.372l + 4ml

5. When painting the kitchen of his house, Tom used a 2.5l tin, a 1l 40ml tin and a 750ml tin. How much paint did he use altogether?

Gloss Paint

6. Out of a 2l carton of milk, the Murphy family drank the following amounts over 2 days: 128ml, $\frac{3}{8}$l, 0.2l and 210ml. How much milk was left in the carton?

7. Now try these subtraction questions. Change capacities to the same unit first.
   a) 9675ml – 1.36l
   b) 8l 424ml – 3850ml
   c) 6.95l – 988ml
   d) 9040ml – 1l 58ml
   e) 5l 274ml – 4.12l
   f) 7.7l – 6l 837ml

8. A home heating oil tank was filled to capacity (500l). The following amounts of oil were used over 3 weeks: 29.75l, 17l 540ml and 32.5l. How much oil is left in the tank?

9. Use your calculator to find the capacities. (Remember to convert all capacities to the same unit first.)
   a) 265.8l + 563l 278ml + 129.3l
   b) 28l 26ml + 138.452l + 97.5l
   c) 800l – (238l 460ml + 408.76l)
   d) 569l 6ml – 437.6l
   e) 265.9l – 207l 43ml
   f) (25.62l + 50.75l) – (47l 376ml + 8.4l)

There are a few ways of writing the multiplication and division of capacities too.
Check if you get the same answer for the amount of tomato juice from each question.

a)
```
      ml
     2125
  ×     5
  _____
```

b)
```
   l    ml
   2   125
  ×      5
  _____
```

c)
```
    litres
    2.125
  ×     5
  _____
```

Karen filled her petrol tank with 48.44l of petrol on Monday. By the following Monday her tank was empty. On average, how much petrol did she use each day?

a)
```
       ml
  7 | 48440
```

b)
```
    l    ml
  7 | 48   440
```

c)
```
    litres
  7 | 48.44
```

---

0. The Beguiling Bistro is placing their weekly drinks order with their supplier. Some of the drinks come in containers with an unusual capacity. Calculate how many litres of each item the bistro has ordered.

	Capacity	Number required
Tomato juice	2.125l	5
Orange juice	3l 50ml	9
Grapefruit juice	750ml	6
Apple juice	1.9l	8
Blackcurrant juice	0.521l	4
Lemonade	5.65l	12
Cola	4l 390ml	25
Orangeade	3865ml	32

11. Now try these.

  a) $6.88l ÷ 4$

  b) $7l\ 125ml ÷ 5$

  c) $7800ml ÷ 6$

  d) $17l\ 40ml ÷ 8$

  e) $32.95l ÷ 10$

  f) $10l\ 983ml ÷ 7$

  g) $67.2l ÷ 12$

  h) $8l\ 535ml ÷ 15$

  i) $231.8l ÷ 38$

12. Calculate the total price from the information given.

85c per 500ml

€1.55 per litre

€12 per litre

80c per 600ml

50c per 250ml

€1.20 per 1.5 litres

  a) Cost of 1.5l of cola (500ml = 85c, so 1500ml = 85c × 3 = €_____)

  b) Cost of 3l of orange juice

  c) Cost of $2\frac{1}{2}l$ of paint

  d) Cost of 1200ml of tomato ketchup

  e) Cost of 1l of banana smoothie

  f) Cost of 500ml of mineral water

Homework

1. Can you write these as litres and millilitres?

  a) 2098ml

  b) 1754ml

  c) 4201ml

  d) 1.7l

  e) 3.852l

  f) 6.05l

  g) 560ml

  h) 4.9l

  i) 7.248l

2. Fill in the gaps.

ml	l ml	l
3098ml		
	5l 36ml	
		4.195l
		8.01l
	7l 437ml	

3. Now try these. Remember to change them to the same units before you start.

  a) $9065ml + 3l\ 412ml + 5.342l$

  b) $4.08l + 8001ml + 6l\ 185ml$

  c) $2.63l + 3l\ 79ml + 845ml$

  d) $3l\ 767ml + 3.619l + 4809ml$

  e) $5.286l + 4l\ 4ml + 5361ml$

  f) $8l\ 930ml + 0.539l + 4023ml$

4. Now try these subtraction questions, also changing capacities to the same unit first.

a) 7l 234ml – 1.85l

b) 7003ml – 2l 86ml

c) 9.152l – 3867ml

d) 7l 154ml – 2.957l

e) 6814ml – 5.768l

f) 3l 29ml – 879ml

5. Now try these.

a) 793ml × 8

b) 5l 479ml × 6

c) 3.64l × 9

d) 6l 76ml × 28

e) 6483ml × 19

f) 2.607l × 34

6. Now try these.

a) 7.38l ÷ 9

b) 4l 368ml ÷ 8

c) 9044ml ÷ 7

d) 82.6l ÷ 14

e) 9l 131ml ÷ 23

f) 65.1l ÷ 35

7. What is the total capacity of 48 bottles if each bottle holds 0.625l?

8. If a school water tank has a capacity of 85l 470ml and 24.986l of water is used, how much is left in the tank?

9. If Jenny drank 938ml of water on Monday, 1.02l on Tuesday and 1l 89ml on Wednesday, how much water did she drink over the 3 days?

Recap

- I can compare and estimate capacities.

- I can record capacities as litres and millilitres.

- I can add capacities.

- I can subtract capacities.

- I can multiply capacities.

- I can divide capacities.

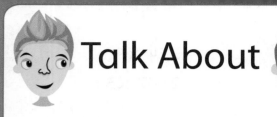 # Talk About

1. a) John's timetable for tomorrow has become a bit mixed up. Can you sort it out for him by placing the events in order and by changing the times from am/pm to the 24-hour clock?

1:15pm	Meet Rebecca for lunch
9:30pm	Go to bed
8:10am	Eat breakfast
3:45pm	Buy groceries in supermarket
10:25am	Get stamps in post office
7:45am	Get up
5:05pm	Eat dinner
5:50pm	Read 3 chapters of latest book
8:35am	Leave the house
7:45pm	Watch some TV

b) How long will John spend watching TV?

c) How long after he gets up will he leave the house?

d) How much time will he spend eating breakfast and dinner?

e) How long after he gets out of bed will it be before he gets back into bed?

2. Change these 24-hour clock times to am or pm.

a) 19:42   b) 06:08   c) 11:13

d) 23:25   e) 17:10   f) 09:45

g) 13:00   h) 12:15   i) 20:20

j) 07:50   k) 00:34   l) 15:48

m) Write down what you were doing yesterday at each of these times.

3. a) If it took Rachel 5 minutes 13 seconds to walk to the shop and it took her only 3 minutes 47 seconds to walk back from the shop, how much quicker was the journey home?

b) Can you suggest a reason why it took longer to walk to the shop?

4. If it took Malcolm 2 hours 56 minutes to make a jigsaw and a further 1 hour 35 minutes to complete a crossword, how long did he spend altogether solving puzzles?

Puzzler

Mike travelled to Moscow from London by plane. He took off at 12:00 noon and arrived at 7:00pm. However, when he arrived he received a message saying he was needed back in London urgently, so he got back on the return flight, which left 1 hour later and took 4 hours to reach London. What time do you think Mike arrived back in London? Talk about it with the people near you. Agree on an answer and then see what others in the class think.

Time Zones

- What time of the day is it now?
- Is it daylight?
- Why is it daylight?
- Will it be daylight in 12 hours' time?
- If not, why not?

- How long does it take the earth to make 1 full rotation on its axis (how long does it take for it to spin around once)?
- Is it exactly the same time everywhere in the world?
- Why might it cause problems in Australia if it was exactly the same time there now as it is in Ireland?

To overcome this difficulty, the world has been divided into **time zones**.

This map of the world shows the different time zones the world is divided into. All places that are between the same pair of lines are at the same time.

1. Find Ireland on the above map.

   a) If it's 12:00 noon in Ireland's time zone, then the time in the next time zone to the east is _____ and the time in the next time zone to the west is _____.

   b) As we travel east, each time zone is 1 hour further _____. As we travel west, each time zone is 1 hour further _____.

   c) Why, do you think, are the lines not straight? What problems would be caused by having straight lines dividing up the time zones?

   d) What problems does a country like the USA have with time zones?

2. Use the map of the time zones and your atlas to help you answer the following questions.

If it's 12:00 in Dublin, what time is it in the following places?

a) New York

b) San Francisco

c) Moscow

d) Berlin

e) Sydney

f) Bangkok

g) London

h) Rio de Janeiro

3. Now try these time puzzles.

a) If it's 14:00 in Oslo, what time is it in Mumbai?

b) If it's 21:40 in Beijing, what time is it in Athens?

c) If it's 06:34 in Chicago, what time is it in Vienna?

d) If it's 19:52 in Melbourne, what time is it in Nairobi?

4. If you were travelling to New York from Dublin, your plane took off at 15:00 and the flight took 5 hours, what time would you land in New York?

5. If you were travelling from New York to Dublin, your plane took off at 11:00 and the journey took 6 hours, what time would you land in Dublin?

6. Why might the exact same journey take longer when flying in the opposite direction?

7. a) What unusual thing would happen if you left Australia on a Tuesday travelling east and continued your journey to Hawaii?

b) What would happen if you travelled in the opposite direction?

8. Can you name any 2 places in the world where the times shown on a clock are identical but where one time is am and the other time is pm (in other words, 2 places where the time is exactly 12 hours apart)?

Average Speed

It took Jane 8 seconds to walk from the top of the PE hall to the bottom. If the hall is 24m long, how quickly was she walking?

It's not possible to say exactly how quickly she was walking for every second of the 8 seconds. She may have started slowly and got quicker, or she may have started quickly and begun to run out of steam near the end. But we can work out the average speed at which she walked.

8 seconds = 24 metres
1 second = 3 metres

So we can say that Jane walked at an average speed of 3 metres per second.

1. a) Work out the average speed of the following people on their journeys. Write your answers as metres per second.
       Frank – 84 metres in 12 seconds   Ben – 75 metres in 15 seconds
       Judy – 207 metres in 23 seconds   Natalie – 280 metres in 35 seconds

    b) Whose average speed was the quickest?

    c) Whose average speed was the slowest?

Task:
Measure a distance out in the yard/field with a trundle wheel (30 metres if you have room). Mark the starting point and the finishing point clearly. Use a stopwatch to time how quickly each person in the class covers the 30 metres.

Now construct a table like the one below and calculate the average speed of each person. You can use a calculator to work it out.

Name	Time	Distance	Average speed
Leo	5.12 seconds	30 metres	5.86 metres per second
Bob	5.43 seconds	30 metres	5.52 metres per second
Mary	4.92 seconds	30 metres	6.10 metres per second

Did you know that the speedometer in a car measures how quickly the car is travelling?

If it reads 40km per hour, it's telling you that if you kept travelling at exactly that speed, you would have travelled 40km after 1 hour of driving.

2. a) Work out the average speed of the following people on their journeys. Write your answers as km per hour.

   Tony – 180km in 3 hours   Alice – 150km in 2.5 hours
   Denise – 175km in 3.5 hours   Andrew – 220km in 4 hours
   Jenny – 650km in 1.5 hours

   b) Can you suggest how Jenny was travelling?

3. On 16 August 2009 in Berlin, Jamaican sprinter Usain Bolt broke the world record for the 100 metres that he had set exactly 1 year earlier to the day in the Olympics in Beijing. He lowered the record by $\frac{11}{100}$ of a second, for a time of 9.58 seconds. This made him the fastest man in the world. What was his average speed for the distance?

4. a) 4 days later, Usain Bolt broke his 200m world record, which again he had set 1 year before. His new record time was 19.19 seconds. What was his average speed while setting the world record?

   b) Can you spot anything remarkable when you compare the 2 average speeds?

5. Look up some other world records and see what the average speed achieved was.

Homework

Change these am/pm times to 24-hour clock times.

a) 2:46pm	b) 9:23am	c) 11:13am	d) 8:15pm
e) 12:10am	f) 11:45pm	g) 12:01pm	h) 4:52pm
i) 7:30am	j) 9:22pm	k) 5:29pm	l) 1:17am

Use the map of the time zones and your atlas to help you answer the following questions

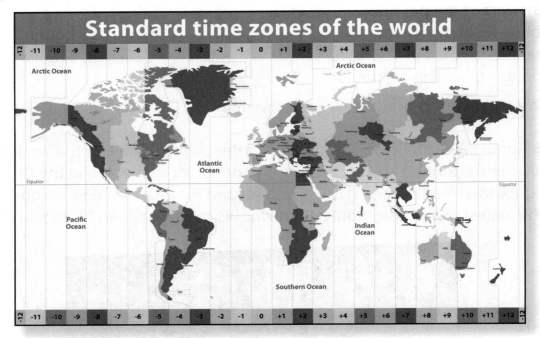

2. How many time zones would you pass through if you travelled from:

   a) Dublin to San Francisco
   b) Melbourne to Cape Town
   c) Paris to Tokyo
   d) Washington to Athens
   e) Copenhagen to Toronto
   f) Rio de Janeiro to Cairo

3. Why are there 2 answers to all of the questions in question 2?

4. Can you work out how far each of these people has travelled?

Name	Average speed	Time travelling	Distance travelled
Sarah	89km/h	4.5 hours	
John	57km/h	6 hours	
Debbie	94km/h	2.5 hours	
Rachel	76km/h	5.5 hours	
Martha	118km/h	3 hours	

Recap

- I can change times from the 12-hour to the 24-hour clock. ○ ○ ○

- I understand why there are time zones. ○ ○ ○

- I can work out the time in different places around the world. ○ ○ ○

- I can work out average speed. ○ ○ ○

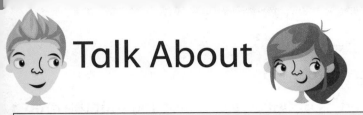

Talk About

Draw a square centimetre (1 cm²) on a piece of paper and cut it out.

Now draw a square whose sides are 2cm long. What is the area of this square? Cut it out and put it beside the square centimetre.

This time, draw a square whose sides are 5cm long. What is the area of this square? Cut it out and put it beside the others.

Now draw a square whose sides are 10cm long. What is the area of this square? Cut it out and put it beside the others.

In a suitable place, draw a square metre (m²) in chalk on the ground. Use a metre stick to help you. How long will each of the sides of the square be in centimetres? Work out what the area of the square metre is in cm². Now put the other squares you have drawn beside the square metre and compare them in size.

Complete this sentence:

$$1 m^2 = \underline{\hspace{2cm}} cm^2$$

Ares and Hectares

When finding the area of larger spaces, we can use larger units of measurement.

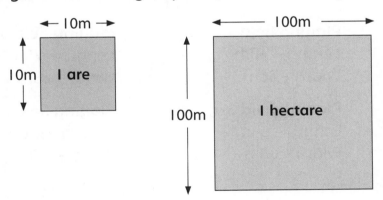

The area of a basketball court or a small car park would be measured in **ares**. The area of a small park/green or 2 football pitches side by side would be measured in **hectares**.

Suggest 3 surfaces whose area could be measured in **ares** and 3 surfaces whose area could be measured in **hectares**.

Complete the following mathematical sentences:

1 are = _____m²

1 hectare = _____m²

Can you suggest how many ares make up a hectare?

If the area of a basketball court is measured as **400m²**, we can also say that the area of the court is **4 ares**.

1. What is the area of a tennis court in ares if its area is measured as 350m²?

2. Change these area amounts from m² to ares.

   a) 700m² = _____ ares　　b) 1300m² = _____ ares　　c) 250m² = _____ ares

   d) 375m² = _____ ares　　e) 1496m² = _____ ares　　f) 87m² = _____ ares

3. Now calculate the area of each of the following playing fields. Record the area in ares.

   Playing field 1
   Length – 25m
   Width – 20m

   Playing field 2
   Length – 40m
   Width – 36m

   Playing field 3
   Length – 75m
   Width – 43m

   Playing field 4
   Length – 132m
   Width – 27m

   Playing field 5
   Length – 84m
   Width – 68m

   Playing field 6
   Length –156m
   Width – 48m

Puzzler

Can you name and give the dimensions of any 2-D shape where the value of the area of the shape is exactly equal to the value of its perimeter?

4. a) Farmer Ruth has just ploughed 1 of her fields. If the field is 150m long and 80m wide, what is the area of the field in m²?

   b) How would you write this measurement in hectares?

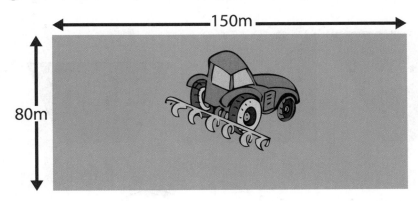

5. Calculate the area of each of Farmer Ruth's fields. Record the area in hectares.

Field 1
Length – 140m
Width – 75m

Field 2
Length – 130m
Width – 90m

Field 3
Length – 175m
Width – 83m

Field 4
Length – 236m
Width – 65m

Field 5
Length – 294m
Width – 57m

Field 6
Length – 306m
Width – 43m

6. a) Which of Farmer Ruth's fields has the greatest area?

   b) What is the difference in hectares between her largest field and her smallest field?

Area of Irregular Shapes

1. On a piece of tracing paper, draw a rectangle that is 15cm long and 15cm wide. Divide up the rectangle into a grid of square centimetres, like the one below, but with 15 rows.

Now place the grid over the following shapes so that you can make a good estimate at the area of each of the shapes in cm². Count the number of full square centimetres contained in each shape and combine the partial squares to make full square centimetres.

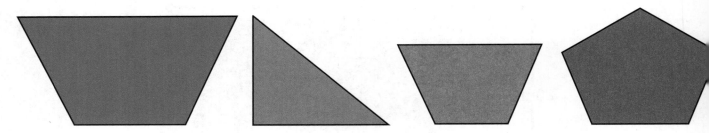

2. What is the difficulty with a circle?

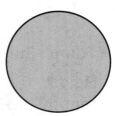

3. Look at this shape. It's made up of rectangles, but can you spot them? We've helped to find 1 of them. Find the others yourself. Copy it into your copy and colour each of the rectangles you find in a different colour. (There is more than one way of dividing up the shape.)

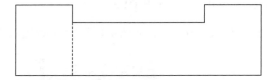

4. Divide this shape into 3 different rectangles. Label the rectangles A, B, and C. Find the area of each of the rectangles.

The total area of the shape is:
area A + area B + area C = ?

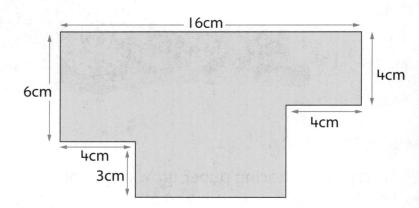

5. If the drawing in question 4 was a plan of a bungalow and it was drawn to a scale of 1cm for every 2.8m, what would be the area of the bungalow in m² and ares?

1. Change these area amounts from m² to ares.
   a) 900m²   b) 1400m²   c) 360m²
   d) 485m²   e) 1728m²   f) 56m²

2. Calculate the area of each of the following playgrounds. Record the area in ares.

   Playground 1   **Playground 2**   **Playground 3**
   Length – 27m   Length – 38m   Length – 64m
   Width – 25m   Width – 30m   Width – 52m

   Playground 4   **Playground 5**   **Playground 6**
   Length – 118m   Length – 78m   Length – 135m
   Width – 26m   Width – 57m   Width – 46m

3. Calculate the area of each of the following parks. Record the area in hectares.

   Park 1   **Park 2**   **Park 3**
   Length – 145m   Length – 150m   Length – 182m
   Width – 75m   Width – 63m   Width – 78m

   Park 4   **Park 5**   **Park 6**
   Length –229m   Length – 284m   Length – 318m
   Width – 57m   Width – 46m   Width – 62m

4. Place a cm² grid over the following shapes so that you can make a good estimate of the area of each of the shapes. Count the number of full square centimetres contained in each shape and combine the partial squares to make full square centimetres.

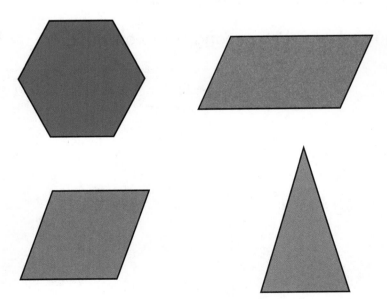

5. Calculate the area of this shape by dividing it into smaller rectangles and working out the area of each.

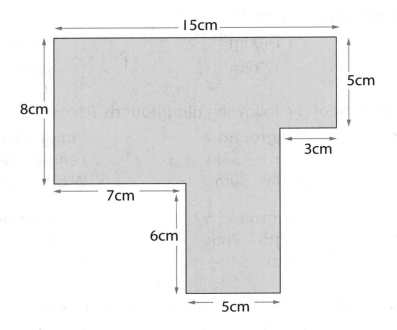